Walking Games and Activities

June Decker, PhD
Western New Mexico University

Monica Mize, PhD
Weber State University

Human Kinetics

Library of Congress Cataloging-in-Publication Data

Decker, June Irene.
    Walking games and activities / by June Decker and Monica Mize.
      p. cm.
    ISBN 0-7360-3430-7
    1. Physical education and training--Study and teaching (Elementary)--United States. 2.
Physical education and training--Study and teaching (Secondary)--United States. 3.
Fitness walking. I. Mize, Monica, 1950- II. Title.

    GV365 .D43 2001
    613.7'176--dc21

                            2001016878

ISBN: 0-7360-3430-7

Acquisitions Editor: Amy Pickering
Developmental Editor: Myles Schrag
Assistant Editors: Amanda S. Ewing, J. Gordon Wilson
Copyeditor: Barbara Field
Proofreader: Sue Fetters
Graphic Designer: Robert Reuther
Graphic Artist: Angela K. Snyder
Cover Designer: Jack W. Davis
Photographer (cover): Tom Roberts
Art Manager: Craig Newsom
Illustrator: Tom Roberts
Printer: Versa

Printed in the United States of America   10 9 8 7 6 5 4 3 2 1

Human Kinetics
Web site: www.humankinetics.com

United States: Human Kinetics
P.O. Box 5076
Champaign, IL 61825-5076
800-747-4457
email: humank@hkusa.com

Canada: Human Kinetics
475 Devonshire Road Unit 100
Windsor, ON N8Y 2L5
800-465-7301 (in Canada only)
e-mail: orders@hkcanada.com

Europe: Human Kinetics, Units C2/C3 Wira Business Park
West Park Ring Road
Leeds LS16 6EB, United Kingdom
+44 (0) 113 278 1708
e-mail: hk@hkeurope.com

Australia: Human Kinetics
57A Price Avenue
Lower Mitcham, South Australia 5062
08 8277 1555
e-mail: liahka@senet.com.au

New Zealand: Human Kinetics
P.O. Box 105-231, Auckland Central
09-523-3462
e-mail: hkp@ihug.co.nz

We dedicate this book to Charles, Virginia, Monty, Cherrie, Harold, and Delene for their love and support, as well as to those who have kept us walking: Markie, Cori, Patches, Pepper, Shonto, and Taz.

Contents

Activity Finder

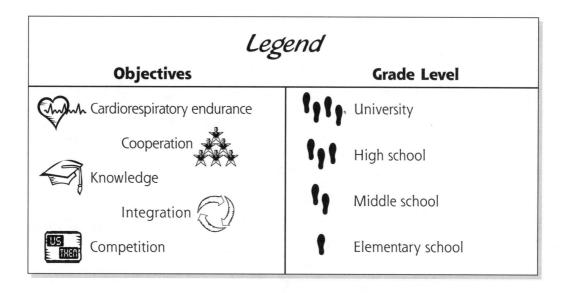

Legend

Objectives	Grade Level
Cardiorespiratory endurance	University
Cooperation	High school
Knowledge	Middle school
Integration	Elementary school
Competition	

Aerobic Games

Name of Game	Page #	Cardiorespiratory endurance	Cooperation	Knowledge	Integration	Competition	University	High school	Middle school	Elementary school
Add 'Em Up for the Team	52	✔	✔			✔	✔	✔	✔	✔
Alphabet Game	54	✔	✔	✔			✔	✔	✔	✔
Around the Town	56	✔	✔			✔	✔	✔	✔	
Calendar Walk	58	✔		✔			✔	✔	✔	✔
Card Walk	62	✔	✔	✔	✔	✔	✔	✔	✔	✔
Conversation Game	65	✔	✔	✔			✔	✔	✔	✔
Design a Route	67	✔		✔	✔		✔	✔		
Destination Walk	69	✔		✔			✔	✔	✔	✔
Double Your Fun	73	✔		✔			✔	✔		
Estimated Pace	76	✔		✔			✔	✔	✔	
15-Minute Paper Clip Walk	78	✔		✔			✔	✔	✔	✔
Find a Friend	81	✔	✔				✔	✔	✔	✔
Grab Bag Workout	83	✔		✔	✔		✔	✔	✔	

Preface

"What are we going to do today?"

How many times have your students asked *that* question?

"Walking!" you reply.

The moans and groans begin.

As teachers and activity leaders, we all know the many lifetime fitness benefits that can be derived from walking. However, we often have trouble convincing our students that walking isn't boring and can actually be fun. These negative opinions can be quickly overcome by using a wide variety of fun and challenging walking games as part of a walking unit. Think how differently the students will respond if you say that we are playing Coyotes and Roadrunners or Beat That Lap. Fitness need not be boring. By taking part in a combination of challenging learning activities and games, students can experience an active workout without even knowing it!

Whether you're an experienced teacher or a novice, whether you deal with elementary students or college students, *Walking Games and Activities* provides a variety of experiences that can be adapted to meet the needs of the broad spectrum of your students. Walking for fitness is a convenient, inexpensive, lifelong, healthy activity that millions of people enjoy as exercise. The intent of this book is to introduce walking as a form of fun and challenging exercise. These activities provide opportunities for cooperation, friendly competition, fitness, and fun for students from upper elementary through college age.

Walking Games and Activities is the first book to combine the concepts of fitness walking and walking activities into one useful resource for teachers and activity leaders. The activities found in *Walking Games and Activities* are easy to teach, practical, and fun for students. The book includes guidelines for you to keep in mind as you add walking to your curriculum, including tips for inclusion and sample walking units for elementary-level through college-age students. Eighteen mini-lectures related to topics such as walking form and nutrition provide context for your students to get started. Forty games designed to enhance fitness give your students the opportunity to have fun while exercising, and each activity is accompanied by a worksheet to make walking more exciting and educational than you ever imagined! Finding the games to suit your specific needs is easy using the Game Finder at the front of the book. Planning time will be reduced because we've provided almost everything you need except the equipment and the students.

Each activity and game in the book contains the following features in an easy-to-follow format:

Type of activity: aerobic, interval, classroom

Objective(s): Cardiorespiratory endurance, knowledge, cooperation, competition, and integration

Safety: Suggestions to make the learning environment safe

Grade level: Appropriate level for activity

Facility: Learning environment best suited for each activity

Equipment: Optimal equipment needed for each activity

Organization: How students will be organized for the activity

Prerequisite: Mini-lecture(s) that complement the games and activities

Teaching instructions: A step-by-step description of the organization, playing area, rules and regulations, scoring procedures, and safety procedures

Worksheet: Reinforcing exercises for students to complete during or at the conclusion of every game, activity, and mini-lecture

Teaching tips: Suggestions that will help the teacher implement the games successfully

Variations: Options that provide variety in how the games may be played

We have used the contents of *Walking Games and Activities* in our classes for years, and our students love them. Graduates of our programs have also used these activities successfully in el-ementary, middle, and high schools with great success. You can too. We hope you have as much fun as we and our students have had with these activities. In writing this book, we have made no effort to prescribe what you should do in your classes. Rather, we have shared ideas that have worked for us. We hope this sparks your creativity, as you can adapt our activities for your specific situation. Happy walking!

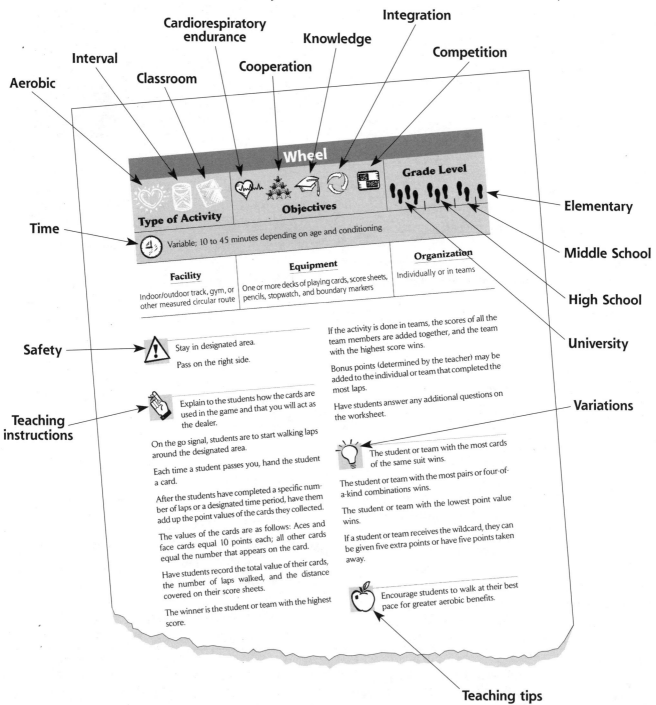

Acknowledgments

Walking Games and Activities became possible only through the encouragement and aid of many individuals. We want to acknowledge Sharon Leslie for countless hours spent preparing the manuscript with care and accuracy and JoAnn Otte for her support, suggestions, and editing. Finally, we are grateful to all of our students for their contributions and ideas and for continually challenging us to become better teachers.

Teaching Guidelines

The purpose of this book is to offer teachers walking games and activities that can be useful within a larger physical education curriculum. The needs and situations in your educational setting may vary dramatically from others, but as you plan your curriculum, you will find the guidelines presented in this chapter valuable. They include safety tips, tips for inclusion, and developmental objectives to keep in mind as you choose appropriate walking games, activities, and mini-lectures for your students. A sample scope and sequence for elementary school, middle school, high school, and college walking units gives you a helpful, flexible framework for adapting these resources to your specific situation.

Safety Tips for Teachers

Although walking is generally a safe activity, there are precautions you should follow when conducting your classes.

- Choose activities that are developmentally appropriate for your students. Even though an activity may be appropriate for the majority of students at a grade level, the maturity of your particular group is an essential consideration.
- Establish a class rule stating that when students are walking a route, they are responsible for the person behind them. This keeps your class together.
- Emphasize that activity rules must be followed. Horseplay and breaking the rules often lead to injuries.
- Be aware of students with health problems. Walking becomes a high-intensity activity for students with low fitness levels.
- Check the route you want to walk by driving it first, if possible.
- Place equipment such as cones for boundaries or jump ropes and mats for circuits strategically to provide maximum safety.
- Inform students of safety precautions that must be followed if activities take place off your campus:

    Walk on the left facing traffic.

    Do not walk in the street if traffic is present.

    Avoid sidewalks with broken concrete or high curbs.

    If dogs bother you, stop and tell them "No!" in a stern voice. Do not run.

    Slow your pace if you begin feeling dizzy.

    Let someone know where you are going.

    Avoid construction sites and congested streets.

    Carry identification.

    Walk with another person or group.

    Wear reflective clothing.

Tips for Inclusion

Many walking activities are appropriate for students with special needs. Here are some general tips:

- Pair special students with a buddy who will help them with the activity.
- Pair visually impaired students with a buddy who will guide them while walking; have each student hold one end of a rope or scarf to keep pairs together.
- Use written instructions for hearing-impaired students.
- Arrange for students in wheelchairs to be pushed by their classmates while participating in activities.
- Establish a common language within the physical education setting regarding boundaries, equipment, start/stop signals, rules, and safety.

- Encourage students to invent ways for all children to participate.
- Make use of upper grade learning buddies.
- Use paraprofessionals.
- Slow the activity pace.
- Lengthen or shorten the time of the activity.
- Provide rest periods.
- Provide safety zones around the learning environment.
- Provide special equipment.
- Be flexible.

Sample Walking Units

Preliminary Considerations

- Determine the length of the class period.
- Determine the grade to be taught.
- Determine the length of the unit.
- Identify the unit objectives.
- Make the unit long enough to accomplish the objectives.
- Choose activities that meet the maturity level of your students. Grade level is not always the best indicator.
- Provide a variety of activities.
- Decide how activities will be presented to ensure a productive learning environment.
- Address all domains of learning: cognition (knowledge), psychomotor (skill), and affective (behavior).
- Build on what the students already know based on previous grade level and units taught.
- Develop a list of equipment, supplies, and facilities needed to implement the unit.
- Determine whether or not students should be allowed to walk off campus.
- Plan a different walking route for each week of class. Walk the route one way one day and reverse the route the next class period.
- Use approximately one game per week to add variety to the classes.
- Remember, there is more to fitness walking than just playing games. The games are for variety, motivation, and change of pace.

Development Objectives

Walking games and activities can be used to reinforce and enhance the development of a walking unit. They can be used at the beginning of a lesson, as the entire lesson, or as a culminating activity at the end of the lesson. At the end of the unit, students should develop the following based on the preliminary considerations that are relevant to your situation:

- Proper walking form
- Responsibility for personal fitness
- Understanding of the benefits of walking as an aerobic activity
- Knowledge to determine target heart rate zone
- Skills to participate in a variety of walking activities
- Ability to work cooperatively with classmates
- Basic understanding of nutrition
- Knowledge of the equipment necessary for fitness walking

Elementary School Sample Unit

Sample Scope and Sequence

Three weeks, three days a week:

Day 1: Benefits of Walking Mini-lecture and Pass Back and Walk Forward

Day 2: Hot Pursuit

Day 3: Safety Mini-lecture and Beat That Lap

Day 4: Nutrition Mini-lecture and Add 'Em Up for the Team

Day 5: Activity of Teacher's Choice

Day 6: Walk Route 1 or Target Heart Rate Mini-lecture

Day 7: Walk Route 2 or Coyotes and Roadrunners

Day 8: Walk Route 3 or Destination Walk

Day 9: Walk Route 3 in Reverse and Activity of Teacher's Choice

Middle School Sample Unit

Sample Scope and Sequence

Three weeks, five days a week:

Day 1: Benefits of Walking Mini-lecture and Conversation Game

Day 2: Walking Pretest and Find a Friend

Day 3: Walking Safety Mini-lecture and Walk Route 1

Day 4: Walking Technique Mini-lecture and Partner Relays

Day 5: Walk Route 2

Day 6: Estimated Pace

Day 7: FIT Principle Mini-lecture and Walk Aerobics

Day 8: Walk Route 1 in Reverse

Day 9: Hot Pursuit

Day 10: M&M Terminator and Catch Your Partner

Day 11: Mile Walk (1.6 km) Test and Nutrition Mini-lecture

Day 12: Grab Bag Workout

Day 13: Partner Relays

Day 14: Walk, Crunch, and Jump Rope

Day 15: Student Choice

4

High School Sample Unit

Sample Scope and Sequence

Six weeks, five days a week:

Day 1: Benefits of Walking Mini-lecture, Conversation Game, Find a Friend, and Target Heart Rate Range

Day 2: Walk Route 1 and Safety Mini-lecture

Day 3: Walk Route 1 in Reverse

Day 4: Walk Route 2 and Walking Technique Mini-lecture

Day 5: Walk Route 2 in Reverse

Day 6: Hot Pursuit

Day 7: Walk Route 3

Day 8: Walk Route 3 in Reverse

Day 9: Catch Your Partner

Day 10: Walk Route 4 and Environmental Concerns Mini-lecture

Day 11: Walk Route 4 in Reverse

Day 12: Walk Route 5 and Nutrition Mini-lecture

Day 13: Walk Route 5 in Reverse

Day 14: Activity of Teacher's Choice

Day 15: Walk Route 6 and Body Composition Mini-lecture

Day 16: Walk Route 6 in Reverse

Day 17: Activity of Teacher's Choice

Day 18: Walk Route 7 and Teacher's Choice Mini-lecture

Day 19: Walk Route 7 in Reverse

Day 20: Activity of Teacher's Choice

Day 21: Walk Route 8 and Teacher's Choice Mini-lecture

Day 22: Walk Route 8 in Reverse

Day 23: Activity of Teacher's Choice

Day 24: Walk Route 9 and Staying on Your Program Mini-lecture

Day 25: Walk Route 9 in Reverse

Day 26: Walk Route 10 and Teacher's Choice Mini-lecture

Day 27: Walk Route 10 in Reverse

Day 28: Activity of Teacher's Choice

Day 29: Aerobic Walking Test

Day 30: Written Test

College-Level Sample Unit

Sample Scope and Sequence

Six weeks, five days a week:

Day 1: Benefits of Walking Mini-lecture, Conversation Game, and Find a Friend

Day 2: Walking Safety Mini-lecture, Walking Technique Mini-lecture, and Walk Route 1

Day 3: Walk Route 1 in Reverse

Day 4: Activity of Teacher's Choice

Day 5: Environmental Conditions Mini-lecture and Walk Route 2

Day 6: Walk Route 2 in Reverse and Nutrition Mini-lecture

Day 7: Activity of Teacher's Choice

Day 8: Body Composition Mini-lecture and Walk Route 3

Day 9: Teacher's Choice Mini-lecture and Walk Route 3 in Reverse

Day 10: Activity of Teacher's Choice

Day 11: Walk Route 4 and Teacher's Choice Mini-lecture

Day 12: Walk Route 4 in Reverse

Day 13: Activity of Teacher's Choice

Day 14: Walk Route 5

Day 15: Walk Route 5 in Reverse

Day 16: Activity of Teacher's Choice

Day 17: Walk Route 6 and Perceived Exertion Mini-lecture

Day 18: Walk Route 6 in Reverse

Day 19: Activity of Teacher's Choice

Day 20: Training Principles Mini-lecture and Walk Route 7

Day 21: Walk Route 7 in Reverse

Day 22: Activity of Teacher's Choice

Day 23: Walk Route 8 and Teacher's Choice Mini-lecture

Day 24: Walk Route 8 in Reverse

Day 25: Activity of Teacher's Choice

Day 26: Walk Route 9

Day 27: Walk Route 9 in Reverse

Day 28: Activity of Teacher's Choice

Day 29: Aerobic Walking Test

Day 30: Written Test

Mini-lectures

The mini-lectures in this chapter are designed to help you provide students the information that comprises the fitness walking knowledge base. Each mini-lecture takes only 5 to 10 minutes at the beginning or end of a lesson and should supplement, not substitute for, the actual fitness walking activities. The mini-lectures provide an outline of the key points and/or concepts relevant to each lecture topic. Please choose lectures covering information that is consistent with and relevant to your objectives for teaching fitness walking.

Adjusting to the Environment

Objectives

Understand which environmental factors influence your walking

Understand how environmental conditions influence clothing choice

Understand how environmental conditions influence route selection

Understand how environmental conditions influence when you walk

Adjustments for the Environment

Heat

Dress in light-colored, loose-fitting clothing.

Choose fabrics that "breathe."

Walk during the coolest times of the day. Early morning is best; evening is second best.

Drink water every 15 to 20 minutes.

Walk at a lower intensity (lower heart rate).

Wear sunscreen.

Wear a cap with a bill long enough to shade your eyes.

Choose flatter, less hilly routes.

Avoid walking when the temperature and humidity are both high.

Cold

Dress in dark, loose-fitting layers of clothing. As you walk, your body generates heat, so you will probably want to remove layers as your workout progresses.

Choose fabrics that "breathe."

Walk during the warmest time of the day. Between 2:00 and 4:00 P.M. is best.

Drink water every 15 to 20 minutes.

Warm up adequately before increasing intensity.

Avoid contact with cold objects. Don't sit on walls, touch metal poles, and so forth.

Wear a cap and gloves or mittens.

Choose a route so you will finish with the wind at your back.

Avoid walking when the temperature is low and the wind speed is high.

Adjusting to the Environment Worksheet

Name: _____ **Class:** _____ **Date:** _____

Questions

1. Look through the clothes you have at home. What would you wear when walking in cold weather?

2. What would you wear when walking in hot weather?

3. What other clothing do you need to be able to walk in all types of weather?

From *Walking Games and Activities* by June Decker and Monica Mize, 2002, Champaign, IL: Human Kinetics.

Benefits of Fitness Walking

Objective

Understand the benefits of walking for fitness

Health and Fitness

Walking is a low-impact exercise (easy on the body, helps prevent injury).

Walking improves cardiorespiratory endurance.

Walking improves muscular endurance.

Walking improves flexibility.

Walking can serve as a means of rehabilitation for injury and/or illness.

Walking activities promote effective weight control.

Walking introduces beginners to a physical activity.

Walking can serve as a lead-up to more vigorous physical activities.

Accessibility

Walking techniques are easy to learn.

Walking for exercise is inexpensive.

Walking for exercise is individually convenient.

Walking can be done all year long.

Walking can be done any time of day.

Walking requires very little special equipment.

Walking requires no special court or playing field.

Walking can be done for any length of time to fit into one's schedule.

Walking can be done anywhere.

Social

Walking can be done alone, with a partner, or in a group.

Walking is fun.

Walking is a way of relieving stress.

Walking provides for quality time with family and friends.

Walking is appropriate for all ages and abilities.

Benefits of Fitness Walking Worksheet

Name: _____ **Class:** _____ **Date:** _____

Questions

1. Describe five reasons you would choose walking as an exercise from the list provided in the mini-lecture.

2. What are other reasons you might choose walking as a form of exercise?

From *Walking Games and Activities* by June Decker and Monica Mize, 2002, Champaign, IL: Human Kinetics.

Caloric Expenditure

Objectives

Understand the terms calorie and energy expenditure

Understand how to convert pounds to kilograms

Understand how to calculate calories burned while walking

Points of Caloric Expenditure

Calorie: A unit of measure for energy.

The body's energy needs depend on factors such as body size, body composition, age, and type and amount of exercise.

The heart rate during exercise is a direct reflection of the intensity of the activity and the increased energy expenditure over that expended during rest.

An increase in heart rate is an increase in caloric output.

The energy released during muscle contraction is known as the energy expenditure.

The more time you spend at an activity, the more energy you use.

Higher intensity activities require more energy than lower intensity activities.

Larger people tend to require more energy for the same task than smaller people do.

Activities involving a large amount of muscle mass burn more calories than those involving limited muscle mass. For example, jumping jacks require greater muscle mass than do ankle flexions.

One pound of body weight equals .45 kilograms.

The number of calories burned per minute while walking is equal to .0794 times body weight in kilograms.

Other Activities

Examples of calories burned per hour in other activities are as follows:

Basketball: 642

Tennis: 276

Golf: 216

Sleeping: 60

Caloric Expenditure Worksheet

Name: _____ **Class:** _____ **Date:** _____

1. Record body weight.

2. Convert body weight from pounds to kilograms.

Body weight in pounds _____ times 0.45 equals body weight in kilograms _____

3. Calculate the number of calories burned per minute while walking based on body weight.

0.0794 times body weight in kilograms _____ equals number of calories burned per minute while walking _____

4.

a. How many calories would you burn in a 20-minute walk?

b. How many calories would you burn in a 40-minute walk?

c. How many calories would you burn in a 60-minute walk?

5. How many calories would you burn if you walked three days a week for 40 minutes each day?

From *Walking Games and Activities* by June Decker and Monica Mize, 2002, Champaign, IL: Human Kinetics.

Choosing a Route

Objectives

Understand the importance of choosing appropriate walking routes

Understand how to choose appropriate walking routes

Why Choosing a Route Is Important

Safety

Level of conditioning

Convenience

How to Choose a Walking Route

Safety Considerations

Traffic: Choose routes with as little traffic as possible.

Crown of road: The crown is the curved surface of the road and is created so water will drain off the road. Walking on roads with greatly elevated crowns is difficult and can cause injury because one foot is always higher than the other. Therefore, avoid roads with severe crowns.

Isolation: Choose routes that are well traveled by other people. Avoid walking all by yourself. When possible, walk with a partner or in a group.

Time of day: Avoid walking at night. It's hard for drivers to see you, and it's hard for you to see where you're going.

Surface: Avoid walking on rough, uneven surfaces. You are less likely to become injured on smooth surfaces. If you walk on dirt trails or roads, choose routes that are as free of rocks as possible.

Dogs: Avoid routes where there are unfenced dogs.

Other Considerations

Level of conditioning: If you are in good condition, choose routes that will be challenging for you. Add hills and distance to make walks more difficult. If you aren't very fit yet, choose flatter, shorter routes.

Convenience: Choose routes that are close to home, school, or work. If you have to travel to exercise, you probably will not do it.

Choosing a Route Worksheet

Name: _____ **Class:** _____ **Date:** _____

Map out a route in your neighborhood, where you work, or at school that you might continue to use outside of the physical education class. Include the following information:

1. Written directions of the route

2. Map diagram of the route

3. Distance of the route

4. Evaluation of the route in terms of difficulty, noise, traffic, walking surface, and safety

5. Personal comments about the route

From *Walking Games and Activities* by June Decker and Monica Mize, 2002, Champaign, IL: Human Kinetics.

Choosing a Route Evaluation

Name: _____ **Class:** _____ **Date:** _____

Questions

1. Evaluate the route you walked today based on the items discussed in the mini-lecture at the beginning of the class.

2. How would you change the route to make it better?

From *Walking Games and Activities* by June Decker and Monica Mize, 2002, Champaign, IL: Human Kinetics.

Choosing Equipment

Objective

Understand the appropriate equipment needed for walking for fitness

Equipment

Shoes

Shoes should have a well-cushioned heel cup.

Shoes should be flexible at the ball of the foot.

Shoes should be made of breathable material such as nylon mesh.

Shoes should be comfortable.

Shoes should be lightweight.

Shoes should fit snugly at the heel.

Shoes should provide room for the toes.

Shoes should be of good quality.

Shoes should be used only for walking.

Shoes should always be kept clean and aired out.

Shoes should provide appropriate traction on the walking surface.

Shoes should be specific to the walking activity (street or trail).

Shoes should be purchased for function, not fashion.

Socks

Socks should be appropriately padded in heel and arch based on type of walking activity.

Socks should provide for moisture management.

Socks should be made of acrylic and cotton fibers.

Socks should keep feet cool and dry.

Socks should have spandex in the cuffs to decrease slipping.

Socks should fit snugly to help prevent blisters and friction.

Socks should be designed with a flat seam construction.

Timing Devices

Timing devices include digital watches and stop watches.

Timing devices should be easy to read.

Timing devices should be convenient to carry.

Timing devices should be easy to use.

Water Carriers

Water carriers should be lightweight.

Water carriers should be easy to access.

Water carriers should fit comfortably around the waist or on the back.

Water carriers should have pop-open tops.

Water carriers should have large mouths for easy filling.

Optional Equipment

Heart rate monitor: To monitor working at a beneficial aerobic fitness level

Pedometer: To measure the distance walked

Walkman: To listen to music as a means of entertainment and relaxation during walking

Gear bag: To carry first-aid items, keys, and extra clothing

Sunglasses: To protect eyes from sunrays

Walking stick: To assist the individual while walking

Reflective materials: For safety so that the individual can be seen while walking

Equipment Worksheet

Name: _____ **Class:** _____ **Date:** _____

Complete one of the two assignments listed below:

1. Read an article from a professional journal discussing some aspect of the equipment discussed in the mini-lecture.

   Title of the article:

   Journal, date, volume, page numbers:

   Summary of the article's content:

   Was the information presented in this article useful to you? Why or why not?

2. Visit a sporting goods store and collect information on three different types of walking shoes, two different types of socks, two different types of timing devices, and one additional walking accessory. Summarize the information collected and attach any information obtained.

   Shoes:

   a.

   b.

   c.

   Socks:

   a.

   b.

   Timing Devices:

   a.

   b.

   Other Accessories:

   a.

   General comments on information received:

From *Walking Games and Activities* by June Decker and Monica Mize, 2002, Champaign, IL: Human Kinetics.

FIT Principle

Objectives

Understand the FIT Principle

Apply the FIT Principle

What Is FIT?

FIT is a formula used to describe the frequency, intensity, and length of time you need to participate in an activity for that activity to produce benefits.

F stands for frequency, which means how often you do the activity. Frequency is the number of days per week that you participate in the activity. The recommended frequency for achieving the benefits of walking is three to six days a week.

I stands for intensity, which means how hard you perform the activity. The intensity must be greater than that required for normal daily activities. You must work at an intensity that raises your heart rate into the target zone of 60 to 90 percent of maximum.

T stands for time, which means how long you do the activity. The activity must be done for an effective amount of time for benefits to result. The recommended minimum amount of time for participating in aerobic activities such as walking is 30 minutes.

An example walking program would be to participate in the activity four days a week, working within your target heart rate zone of 60 to 90 percent for 35 minutes per day.

FIT Principle Worksheet

Name: _____   **Class:** _____   **Date:** _____

Complete the following activities.

1. Write an example of your FIT program.

2. In the program described above, indicate the following:

Frequency

Intensity

Time

3. Indicate which of the following is an example of frequency, of intensity, and of time:

Walk within target heart rate zone:

Walk five days a week:

Walk for 45 minutes each day:

4. Design three different programs for walking that would adhere to the FIT Principle

Program 1:

Program 2:

Program 3:

From *Walking Games and Activities* by June Decker and Monica Mize, 2002, Champaign, IL: Human Kinetics.

Maintaining Healthy Body Composition

Objectives

Understand why maintaining healthy body composition is important

Understand how to maintain the body composition appropriate for a healthy lifestyle

Why Healthy Body Composition Is Important

Helps prevent cardiovascular disease

Helps prevent injuries

Helps prevent various types of cancer

Helps control respiratory diseases

How to Maintain Healthy Body Composition

Healthy body fat percentages are as follows:

- Females: 16 to 28 percent
- Males: 9 to 20 percent

To maintain current composition, burn as many calories as you take in.

To increase body fat percentage, take in 3,500 calories more than you burn to gain one pound (.45 kilograms) of fat.

To decrease body fat percentage, take in 3,500 calories less than you burn to lose one pound (.45 kilograms) of fat.

To ensure health, lose or gain no more than one pound per week.

Calories burned by walking equal approximately 100 per mile (62 per kilometer).

Best Strategy for Decreasing Body Fat

Reduce caloric intake and increase exercise.

Small changes make a big difference. By eliminating one regular soda a day, eating smaller portions than you currently do, and walking one mile (1.6 kilometers) a day, you will lose a pound (.45 kilograms) a week.

Maintaining Healthy Body Composition Worksheet

Name: _____ **Class:** _____ **Date:** _____

Please check one:

_____ I think my body composition is about right.

_____ I need to decrease my percentage of body fat.

_____ I need to increase my percentage of body fat.

Design a plan combining diet and exercise to accomplish what you checked above.

From *Walking Games and Activities* by June Decker and Monica Mize, 2002, Champaign, IL: Human Kinetics.

Managing Stress

Objectives

Understand the meaning of stress

Understand the causes of stress

Understand the problems caused by stress

Understand the benefits of walking on stress

Stress

Stress is an emotional, mental, and/or physical response to some external demand or event.

Stress is normal.

Individuals react differently to stress.

Many different things can cause stress.

Stress varies in severity from one individual to another.

Stress changes during one's life span depending on individual experiences such as health, death of a loved one, work, and family.

Stress can have physical effects on the body.

Stress can change behavior by making you tired, depressed, irritable, and unmotivated.

Causes of Stress

Many things can cause stress:

Family members

School

Illness

Boredom

Environmental conditions

Injuries

Weight

Time restraints

Failure

Problems Caused or Affected by Stress

High blood pressure

Depression

Heart disease

Indigestion

Low back pain

Headaches

Low resistance to disease

Suicide

Benefits of Walking Related to Stress

Relieves anxiety

Improves sleep

Reduces stress

Promotes positive self-esteem

Helps improve decision making

Improves self-control

Encourages feelings of accomplishment

Promotes appreciation of the outdoors

Promotes feeling better

Other Ways to Reduce Stress

Time management

Progressive relaxation

Setting realistic goals

Meditation

Managing Stress Worksheet

Name: _____ **Class:** _____ **Date:** _____

1. List four things that could be causing stress in your life.

   a.

   b.

   c.

   d.

2. How do you react in stressful situations?

3. What are some things you might do to help relieve the stress?

From *Walking Games and Activities* by June Decker and Monica Mize, 2002, Champaign, IL: Human Kinetics.

Motivation

Objective

Understanding the importance of motivation in continuing your walking activities

Motivation

Motivating factors differ from person to person. Many beginning exercisers drop out during the first six months of their program. A level of motivation must exist for someone to continue in an exercise program on a regular basis.

Ways to Stay Motivated

Focus on the results.

Do not get in the habit of skipping workouts.

Walk to music.

Walk with a family member.

Set reachable goals.

Get support from people around you.

Keep a chart of your activity.

Understand why you are walking.

Find a convenient place to walk.

Develop a personal reward system.

Motivation Worksheet

Name: _____ **Class:** _____ **Date:** _____

Questions

1. Why do you want to walk for exercise?

    a.

    b.

    c.

2. What are your short-range walking goals? (What can you accomplish now?)

3. What are your long-range walking goals? (What do you want to accomplish as your program progresses?)

4. What motivational techniques will you use to help keep you on your walking program?

From *Walking Games and Activities* by June Decker and Monica Mize, 2002, Champaign, IL: Human Kinetics.

Nutrition

Objectives

Understand the six essential nutrients required by the human body

Understand the 80–20 rule relating to nutrition

Understand the Food Guide Pyramid

Six Essential Nutrients

Carbohydrates

The primary sources of energy for the body

Simple: found in candy, soft drinks, desserts

Complex: found in potatoes, rice, pasta, breads; preferable for energy

Should constitute 60 to 65 percent of the diet

Fat

The secondary source of energy for the body; also used to protect the body from injury and disease

Found in meat, dairy products

Should constitute approximately 20 percent of the diet

Protein

Used for growth and rebuilding tissue; not a prime energy source

Should constitute 15 to 20 percent of the diet

Found in meat, dairy products, rice, beans

Vitamins

Used to regulate body functions

Should meet minimum daily requirements (read labels)

Found in a well-balanced diet of carbohydrates, fat, and protein

Examples: Vitamin B, Vitamin C, Vitamin E

Minerals

Used to regulate body functions

Should meet minimum daily requirements (read labels)

Found in a well-balanced diet of carbohydrates, fat, and protein

Used to transport nutrients and waste products; essential for all body functions

Examples: iron, potassium, zinc

Water

Used to transport nutrients and waste products; essential for all body functions

80–20 Rule

If 80 percent of your diet is healthy, the other 20 percent doesn't have to be. The levels of the Food Guide Pyramid help determine what foods to eat in following the 80–20 rule. The first three levels equal the 80 percent in the 80–20 rule; the fourth level equals the 20 percent.

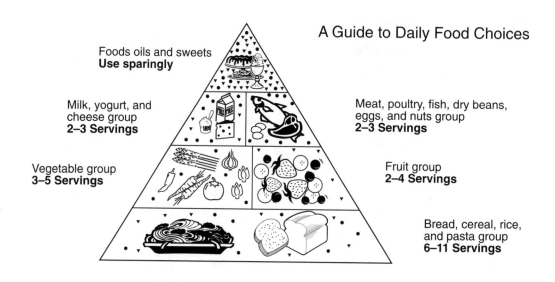

A Guide to Daily Food Choices

Foods oils and sweets
Use sparingly

Milk, yogurt, and cheese group
2–3 Servings

Meat, poultry, fish, dry beans, eggs, and nuts group
2–3 Servings

Vegetable group
3–5 Servings

Fruit group
2–4 Servings

Bread, cereal, rice, and pasta group
6–11 Servings

Key

● Fat (naturally occurring and added)

▼ Sugars (added)

These symbols show fats and added sugars in foods

Level 1

The foundation for your nutrition

Contains 6 to 11 servings of bread, rice, pasta, and cereal

Level 2

Left side contains three to five servings of vegetables

Right side contains two to four servings of fruit

Level 3

Left side contains two to three servings of milk, yogurt, and cheese

Right side contains two to three servings of meat, poultry, eggs, nuts, fish, and dry beans

Level 4

Contains foods high in fat and sugar

Limit consumption of foods in this level to 20 percent

Nutrition Worksheet

Name: _____ **Class:** _____ **Date:** _____

Keep track of your diet for one entire day. Be sure to include all the snacks you eat between meals.

Diet Log

On the following chart, keep track of the foods you eat, the amount eaten, the number of calories, and which food group the food represents.

Breakfast

Food	Amount	Calories	Basic food group

Lunch

Food	Amount	Calories	Basic food group

Dinner

Food	Amount	Calories	Basic food group

Snacks

Food	Amount	Calories	Basic food group

Total calories for the day: _____

From *Walking Games and Activities* by June Decker and Monica Mize, 2002, Champaign, IL: Human Kinetics.

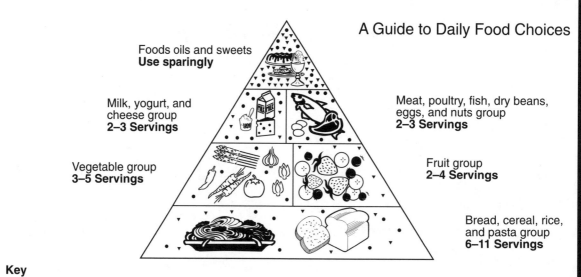

A Guide to Daily Food Choices

Foods oils and sweets
Use sparingly

Milk, yogurt, and
cheese group
2–3 Servings

Meat, poultry, fish, dry beans,
eggs, and nuts group
2–3 Servings

Vegetable group
3–5 Servings

Fruit group
2–4 Servings

Bread, cereal, rice,
and pasta group
6–11 Servings

Key

● Fat (naturally occurring and added)

▼ Sugars (added)

These symbols show fats and added sugars in foods

Record the number of servings you had from each category on the Food Guide Pyramid.

Fats, oils: _____

Fruits: _____

Vegetables: _____

Bread, cereal, pasta: _____

Meat: _____

Questions

1. Discuss your results. In which areas did you meet Pyramid guidelines? In which areas do you need improvement?

2. What specific changes can you make in your diet so you will meet Pyramid guidelines?

From *Walking Games and Activities* by June Decker and Monica Mize, 2002, Champaign, IL: Human Kinetics.

Perceived Exertion

Objectives

Understand the meaning of perceived exertion

Understand why knowledge of perceived exertion is important

What Is Perceived Exertion?

Perceived exertion is awareness of whether you are in your target heart rate range based on how your body feels.

Why Is Perceived Exertion Important?

It isn't always convenient to stop and take your pulse while walking. When you stop walking, your heart rate drops immediately (refer to perceived exertion learning activity), so it's hard to tell when you're actually working at the proper intensity.

Race Walking

Objectives

Understand the history of walking as a competitive activity

Understand the rules governing race walking

Understand proper race walking technique

Demonstrate proper race walking technique

History of Competitive Walking

Pedestrianism

In the late 1800s, men and women competed in walking races of as much as 500 miles (805 kilometers) in length.

Race Walking

Race walking has been an Olympic sport since the early 1900s.

Men compete in 20-kilometer (12.4-mile) and 50-kilometer (31-mile) races at a pace of approximately 3 minutes, 54 seconds per kilometer or 6.5 minutes per mile. Women compete in 10-kilometer (6.2-mile) and 20-kilometer (12.4-mile) races at a pace of approximately 4 minutes, 30 seconds per kilometer or 7.5 minutes per mile.

Rules of race walking

Loss of contact (lifting): One foot must be touching the ground at all times.

Bent knee (creeping): When you take a step, your knee must be straight when your heel hits the ground. It must remain straight until your body weight is directly above that leg.

Race walking technique

Keep trunk straight with shoulders above hips.

Bend arms at 90-degree angles.

Keep head up with eyes looking straight ahead.

Move arms in opposition with legs.

Pull back with arms, producing less force on forward motion. On back pull, bring fingers to middle of sides; on forward motion, bring elbows to middle of sides.

Step forward with slightly shorter than normal strides.

As heel hits the ground, straighten knee.

Roll weight along outside of foot, keeping knee straight until body is above leg.

Push off toes.

Race Walking Worksheet

Name: _____ **Class:** _____ **Date:** _____

Questions

1. Walk one lap concentrating on keeping your arms bent at a 90-degree angle. Were you able to keep your arms at the right angle for the whole lap?

2. Walk one lap concentrating on keeping your knees straight from the time your heels hit the ground until you are in the support position. Were you able to do this for the whole lap?

3. Walk one lap trying to keep your arms bent and your knees straight. Were you able to do this for the entire lap?

4. Which muscles did you feel yourself using during race walking?

5. What is the hardest part of race walking for you to do?

From *Walking Games and Activities* by June Decker and Monica Mize, 2002, Champaign, IL: Human Kinetics.

Staying With Your Program

Objectives

Understand how to stay with a walking program

Understand the threats to staying on a walking program

How to Stay on a Program

Choose a regular time to walk.

Find a walking partner.

Set goals to achieve.

Choose clothing to be used only for walking.

Use a variety of walking routes.

Participate in a walking race.

Keep a walking log.

Join a walking club.

Threats to Staying on a Program

Not scheduling a time to walk

Putting off walking until after you've done everything else

Not having a program to follow and goals to work for

Staying With Your Program Worksheet

Name: **Class:**   **Date:**

Which three of the hints for staying on a program will help you the most and why?

1.

2.

3.

From *Walking Games and Activities* by June Decker and Monica Mize, 2002, Champaign, IL: Human Kinetics.

Taking Your Pulse

Objectives

Develop the ability to take your pulse

Identify how different activities affect your heart rate

Taking Your Pulse

The carotid artery is the large artery on both sides of your neck.

Gently place the index and middle fingers of one hand on your carotid artery.

Count the number of times your heart beats in six seconds.

Multiply the number of times your heart beats in six seconds by 10.

The final number is your heart rate in beats per minute.

Example

Number of heartbeats in six seconds = 11

Multiplying 11 by 10 = 110 beats per minute

Taking Your Pulse Worksheet

Name: _____ **Class:** _____ **Date:** _____

Practice taking your pulse and record it below:

Practice 1

Count beats for six seconds = ___

Multiply by 10 = ___

My heart rate = ___

Practice 2

Count beats for six seconds = ___

Multiply by 10 = ___

My heart rate = ___

Take your pulse rate after completing each of the following activities:

Activity 1

Walk slowly around the specified area for two minutes.

Count beats for six seconds: ___

Multiply by 10: ___

Heart rate: ___

Activity 2

Walk as fast as you can around the specified area for one minute.

Count beats for six seconds: ___

Multiply by 10: ___

Heart rate: ___

Activity 3

Rest for two minutes.

Count beats for six seconds: ___

Multiply by 10: ___

Heart rate: ___

Activity 4

Walk up and down a flight of steps or step up and down off an aerobic step for two minutes.

Count beats for six seconds: ___

Multiply by 10: ___

Heart rate: ___

From *Walking Games and Activities* by June Decker and Monica Mize, 2002, Champaign, IL: Human Kinetics.

Target Heart Rate Zone

Objectives

Determine your target heart rate zone

Develop an understanding for why you need to exercise so your heart rate is in your target heart rate zone

Why Is Target Heart Rate Important?

Your heart rate needs to be in the target zone to improve cardiovascular endurance.

To achieve the benefits of a walking activity, your heart rate needs to be within your target heart rate zone.

Your target heart rate zone is dependent on your age.

The safe zone for exercise is for your heart rate to be between your low (60 percent) and high (90 percent) target heart rate limits.

Your heart rate should not go above the 90 percent limit.

To achieve aerobic benefits, you need to exercise in your target zone at least three times a week for at least 20 minutes.

Procedure for Determining Your Individual Target Heart Rate Zone

To determine the low limit (60 percent):
Subtract your age from 220. This result is called your maximum heart rate.

Multiply that number by .60.

That number equals your lower target heart rate zone.

To determine the high limit (90 percent):
Subtract your age from 220.

Multiply that number by .90.

That number equals your higher target heart rate zone.

Target Heart Rate Procedure Example

The following shows the target heart rate zone for a 16-year-old:

Low limit	*High limit*
220	220
minus 16 (subtract age)	minus 16 (subtract age)
equals 204 (which is the maximum heart rate)	equals 204
times .60 (multiply by .60)	times .90 (multiply by .90)
equals 122.4 (round off to the nearest number: 122)	equals 183.6 (round off to the nearest number: 184)

The heart rate for a 16-year-old should be at least 122 beats per minute and not more than 184 beats per minute to achieve cardiorespiratory benefits.

Target Heart Rate Zone Worksheet

Name: _____ **Class:** _____ **Date:** _____

Take your pulse after completing each of the following activities.

Activity 1

Jump rope for two minutes.

Count heartbeats for six seconds: ___

Multiply by 10: ___

Heart rate at end of activity: ___

Rest for two minutes.

Activity 2

Shoot free throws for two minutes.

Count heartbeats for six seconds: ___

Multiply by 10: ___

Heart rate at end of activity: ___

Rest for two minutes.

Activity 3

Dribble a soccer ball around the gym for two minutes

Count heartbeats for six seconds: ___

Multiply by 10: ___

Heart rate at end of activity: ___

Rest for two minutes.

Activity 4

Shoot layups for two minutes.

Count heartbeats for six seconds: ___

Multiply by 10: ___

Heart rate at end of activity: ___
Rest for two minutes

From *Walking Games and Activities* by June Decker and Monica Mize, 2002, Champaign, IL: Human Kinetics.

(continued)

Put the four activities in order, with 1 being the activity when your heart rate was the fastest and 4 when your heart rate was the slowest:

1.

2.

3.

4.

Calculate your target heart rate zone:

   220 minus your age = _____ times .60 = _____ (lower limit)

   220 minus your age = _____ times .90 = _____ (higher limit)

Did you reach your lower limit target heart rate in any of the four activities you completed? If yes, which ones?

Describe what you learned about your heart rate and different activities:

From *Walking Games and Activities* by June Decker and Monica Mize, 2002, Champaign, IL: Human Kinetics.

Training Principles

Objectives

Identify the five principles of physical training

Understand what each of the five principles of physical training means

Training Principles

Overload

Progression

Specificity

Reversibility

Diminishing returns

What Do the Principles Mean?

Overload: You must do more exercise than you normally do to improve in fitness.

Progression: As you continue in a fitness program, your workload must increase if you are to continue to improve.

Specificity: You get what you train. If you lift weights for your upper body, your upper body will get stronger but your lower body will not. If you stretch your lower back muscles, they will improve in flexibility; the rest of your body will not.

Reversibility: Use it or lose it. If you begin an exercise program and quit, you will lose your fitness gains.

Diminishing returns: The more fit you are, the harder it is to make big improvements.

Training Principles Worksheet

Name: _____ **Class:** _____ **Date:** _____

Design a three-day-a-week walking workout program using at least four principles of training. Explain how you used each principle.

From *Walking Games and Activities* by June Decker and Monica Mize, 2002, Champaign, IL: Human Kinetics.

Walking Technique

Objective

Understand the basic techniques of proper walking form (Refer to the Walking Form Evaluation activity.)

Reasons for Correct Form

Prevent injury

Increase walking speed

Proper Technique

Foot motion

- Make heel contact at 45 degrees to the ground
- Point toes straight ahead
- Carry weight on outside of foot
- Push off of toes
- Keep back straight
- Stand tall
- Align shoulders over hips
- Hold stomach in
- Swing arms in opposition to legs
- Keep hands relaxed
- Keep eyes focused approximately 15 feet (approximately 5 meters) ahead

Walking Warm-Up and Cool-Down

Objectives

Understand the purpose of warming up and cooling down in an activity program

Learn a variety of warm-up and cool-down activities

Warm-Up

Light to moderate activity and stretching done prior to a workout

Why Warm Up?

Prepare the body for activity

Improve performance

Reduce risk of injury

Increase heart rate gradually

Increase blood flow to working muscles

Increase body temperature

Prepare mind and focus attention

How to Warm Up

Make it a daily habit.

Warm up for 5 to 10 minutes.

Do gentle static stretching.

Breathe while stretching.

Stretch each major muscle group.

Walk at a slow to moderate pace.

Areas of the Body to Warm Up and Cool Down

Shoulders

Calves

Abdomen

Thighs

The warm-up should consist of exercises that enhance muscular strength, muscular endurance, flexibility, and aerobic capacity.

Cool-Down

Moderate to light activity and stretching done after a workout

Why Cool Down?

Allow the body to recover from exercise

Decrease the heart rate gradually

Aid in returning blood from the extremities to the heart

Decrease muscle temperature

Reduce the risk of injury

Prevent muscle soreness

Improve flexibility

Relaxation

How to Cool Down

Cool down for 8 to 10 minutes.

Walk, decreasing from a moderate to slow pace.

Stretch each joint and major muscle group.

Walking Warm-Up and Cool-Down Sample Exercises

The following are exercises that can be used for warming up and cooling down.

Flexibility for Back of Neck

Press shoulders down.

Lower chin toward middle of chest.

Hold for 10 seconds, then release.

Lower chin toward middle of chest.

Turn head to the left.

Hold for 10 seconds, then release.

Lower chin toward middle of chest.

Turn head to the right.

Hold for 10 seconds, then release.

Repeat sequence three times.

With head facing front, lean your right ear toward your right shoulder.

Hold for 10 seconds, then release.

With head facing front, lean your left ear toward your left shoulder.

Hold for 10 seconds, then release.

Repeat sequence three times.

Flexibility for Shoulders

Raise both shoulders toward your ears.

Hold for 10 seconds.

Lower both shoulders.

Repeat three times.

Muscular Strength for Shoulders

In prone position with your hands about shoulder-width apart and feet together, push your body up by extending your arms, keeping your back and legs in a straight alignment. Lower your body and repeat three times.

Rest for 10 seconds.

Repeat three times.

Flexibility for Back

Lie on your back and raise your knees to a 90-degree angle.

Grab the back of one thigh with both hands.

Pull the thigh toward your chest, keeping your knee bent.

Switch legs and repeat three times on each leg.

Lie on your back with your knees bent at a 90-degree angle.

Press your lower back to the ground.

Hold for 10 seconds.

Repeat three times.

Flexibility for Trunk

Sit with your right leg extended and your left leg bent and crossed over your right knee.

Place your right arm on the left side of your left leg and push against that leg.

Turn your trunk as far as possible to the left.

Place your left hand on the floor behind your buttocks.

Stretch, reverse, and repeat on the opposite side.

Repeat sequence three times.

Standing, place your right hand on your right hip and stretch your left arm upward and over the right side of your body.

Hold for 10 seconds.

Reverse arms and repeat.

Repeat sequence three times on each side.

Flexibility for Thighs

Stand on your right leg.

Bend your left leg at the knee.

Grasp your left ankle with your left hand, knee pointed down.

Bend your left heel toward your buttocks.

Hold for 10 seconds.

Repeat sequence standing on your left leg.

Repeat sequence three times.

Muscular Strength for Maximum Vertical Jump

Standing beside a wall, perform a maximum vertical jump.

Repeat three times.

Flexibility for Calves

Stand facing a wall with your feet two to three feet (60 to 90 centimeters) away.

Step forward on your left foot to allow both hands to touch the wall.

Keep the heel of your right foot on the ground.

Keep your right knee straight.

Keep your buttocks tucked in.

Lean forward by bending your front knee and arms; hold for 10 seconds.

Switch legs and repeat three times on each leg.

Flexibility for Ankles

Standing on your right foot, lift your left foot off the ground and rotate your ankle clockwise five rotations, then counterclockwise five rotations.

Repeat three times with each foot.

Stand holding your arms out to the sides for balance and raise up on your toes.

Hold for 10 seconds, then return to the starting position.

Repeat three times.

Muscular Endurance for Abdomen

Lie on your back with your knees bent, your feet close to your buttocks, and your arms folded across your chest.

Curl up until your shoulder blades lose contact with the floor.

Return to the starting position and repeat three times.

Place your hands on the floor beside your hips.

Bend your knees at a 90-degree angle.

Pull your knees toward your chest.

Lower your feet and legs almost to the floor.

Repeat three times.

Aerobic Capacity for Other Warm-Up Activities

Walking

Jogging

Jumping rope

Intervals

Walking Warm-Up/Cool-Down Worksheet

Name: **Class:**   **Date:**

Warming up the body for working out and cooling down after working out are very important. Warm-ups and cool-downs help you perform better and help prevent injuries. You can warm up and cool down in many different ways, but remember to warm up and cool down the entire body.

- Design your own personal warm-up and cool-down routine.
- Write the name of the exercise, the purpose of the exercise (endurance, strength, flexibility, or aerobic), the number of repetitions or duration for executing the activity, and identify the body areas that are being warmed up or cooled down.
- Execute your warm-up and cool-down routine and write your personal comments about the effectiveness of the routines below.

Warm-Up

Name of exercise	Purpose	No. of reps/time	Body area

Cool-Down

Name of exercise	Purpose	No. of reps/time	Body area

Personal Comments:

From *Walking Games and Activities* by June Decker and Monica Mize, 2002, Champaign, IL: Human Kinetics.

Walking Games and Activities

The games in this chapter are divided into two main sections: aerobic and interval. They are designed to provide a change of pace and more fun for your fitness walking classes. The games are intended to supplement, not substitute for, the regular fitness walking activities. Each game involves either continuous aerobic walking or interval walking, which in turn leads to the achievement of additional objectives such as cardiorespiratory endurance, knowledge, cooperation, integration, and competition. Each game listing includes its activity type (either aerobic, interval, or classroom), intended objectives, safety tips, recommended grade levels, time required, recommended facilities, necessary equipment, game organization, prerequisite mini-lectures, teaching instructions, variations, and a worksheet. The games are accompanied by worksheets to give students an opportunity for application and reflection. In addition, several classroom activities are provided for rainy days or shortened schedules. Please choose the games and activities that best suit your situation relative to the students, facilities, and environment. Although each game is designed with learning objectives, do not forget the primary purposes: fitness and fun.

Add 'Em Up for the Team

Type of Activity	 Objectives	Grade Level 

 Variable; 10 to 45 minutes depending on age level, conditioning, and time available.

Facility	Equipment	Organization
Indoor/outdoor track, gymnasium, or designated walking route	Pencil and worksheet per team, stopwatch, and boundary markers	Teams

 Stay in designated area or route.

Be aware of other participants.

 Organize students into teams. Everyone is to walk at the same time, so team size is dependent on the number of students in the class; however, you need two or more on a team.

Have team members write their names on the worksheet.

Instruct students to begin walking. Make sure they realize their laps will go toward the team total.

Have team members complete the activity and then record the total number of laps walked on the worksheet.

The winning team is the team with the highest total.

Organize students into teams with equal ability to make the activity more competitive.

Give students paper clips, straws, or bingo chips to help them keep track of the number of laps walked.

Add 'Em Up for the Team Worksheet

Name: _____ **Class:** _____ **Date:** _____

Please provide the following information and answers to the questions:

Names of team members   **Number of laps walked**

1.

2.

3.

4.

5.

Total number of laps for your team:

Questions

1. How could you motivate yourself to walk more laps?

2. How could you work together as a team to walk more total laps?

3. Did you enjoy this activity? Why or why not?

From *Walking Games and Activities* by June Decker and Monica Mize, 2002, Champaign, IL: Human Kinetics.

Alphabet Game

Type of Activity	Objectives	Grade Level

🕐 Entire class period

Facility	Equipment	Organization
Outdoor or indoor walking routes	Alphabet sheets, pencils	Pairs

 Stay in designated area.

Stay with partner.

 Organize students into pairs.

Have students walk a designated route. Tell them to be very observant while walking.

On completion of walking, have each pair identify one item they actually saw starting with each letter of the alphabet. Spelling must be correct.

Have students share their list with their classmates.

Anyone in class can challenge any item. If a challenge is issued, the pair listing the item must tell where they saw it.

 Give students the alphabet sheet before they begin walking and have them identify items as they walk. This works well with younger students. Also, allow students to use one adjective starting with the appropriate letter with words.

 Separate teams from each other when they fill out the worksheets so that they cannot hear anyone else's answers.

Alphabet Game Worksheet

Name: _____ **Class:** _____ **Date:** _____

Record one item you actually saw during the walk starting with each letter of the alphabet. Spelling must be correct

A   N

B   O

C   P

D   Q

E   R

F   S

G   T

H   U

I   V

J   W

K   X

L   Y

M   Z

Questions

1. What made this game difficult?

2. What letters were the hardest to find?

3. What did you learn from this game?

From *Walking Games and Activities* by June Decker and Monica Mize, 2002, Champaign, IL: Human Kinetics.

Around the Town

Type of Activity	Objectives	Grade Level

Entire class period

Facility	Equipment	Organization
Five ourdoor or indoor walking routes of varying distances	Route maps, team point sheet, and worksheet	Teams of five

Stay on course.

Organize students into teams of five. Each team should be as equal as possible to every other team in walking speed.

Give each team copies of the five routes.

Each team chooses which member will walk each route.

On the start signal, all students are to walk their designated route as fast as possible.

The first person to finish each route earns one point for the team, the second to finish earns two points,

the third earns three points, the fourth earns four points, and the fifth earns five points.

The team with the fewest total points is the winner.

For large classes, have students walk in pairs instead of individually.

Encourage students to choose routes based on the best interests of the team, not just on personal preference.

Around the Town Team Point Sheet

	Team 1	Team 2	Team 3	Team 4	Team 5
Route 1					
Route 2					
Route 3					
Route 4					
Route 5					
TOTAL					

Around the Town Worksheet

Name: **Class:**   **Date:**

Questions

1. Did you walk faster or slower than you usually do? Why?

2. Did you enjoy being part of a team? Why or why not?

3. How did your team decide who would walk each route?

4. Did your team make good decisions about who should walk each route? Please explain.

From *Walking Games and Activities* by June Decker and Monica Mize, 2002, Champaign, IL: Human Kinetics.

Calendar Walk

Type of Activity	Objectives	Grade Level

 Variable depending on activity

Facility	Equipment	Organization
Variable depending on distance of walk, age, and conditioning	Dependent on choice of activity; proper shoes, clothing, water carrier	Individual

 Stay in designated area.

Be aware of others around you.

Be aware of traffic.

Make sure you can be seen.

 Give students a copy of the calendar with suggested activities.

Have students choose a minimum of three activities a week to complete.

Have students initial which activities they completed on the calendar and write their personal reactions to the activities below the calendar.

"Choose your walk" is available once each week. Students write their walk choice onto the calendar; on those days they may do a walk of their choice.

Give the students a blank calendar and let them write in the walking activities they intend to do for that month.

Talk to your students about the places they may walk during the week and on weekends to determine a variety of activities to put on the calendar.

Calendar Walk Sample Worksheet

Name: _____ **Class:** _____ **Date:** _____

Sunday	Monday	Tuesday	Wednesday	Thursday	Friday	Saturday
			Walk in place while you watch your favorite TV show	Walk to the grocery store		Choose your walk
Talk a sunrise walk		Walk your dog	Walk to lunch		Choose your walk	Walk the golf course instead of riding in cart
Go for a Sunday walk	Walk your kids to school	Choose your walk		Walk to work	Walk up and down a hill	Park a block from the mall and walk
Walk to church		Walk the stairs instead of taking the elevator	Choose your walk	Walk for 15 minutes up and down the stairs at home	Take a sunset walk.	Challenge walk—go three miles (4.8 kilometers) or 45 minutes
Join a friend for an early morning walk	Choose your walk					

From *Walking Games and Activities* by June Decker and Monica Mize, 2002, Champaign, IL: Human Kinetics.

(continued)

(continued)

Initial the activities you completed.

Write your personal reviews about the activities.

If you select a "choose your walk" day, then describe the walk you choose to do.

Sample Activities

Walk instead of riding your bike.

Walk in a charity walk.

Take a historical walk around the new town you are visiting.

While watching TV, walk around the house during each commercial.

Take a walk with a friend.

Go for a daily family walk.

Walk to your friend's house instead of calling on the phone.

Get off the bus a few blocks from your destination and walk the rest of the way.

Walk the long way home or to the store, church, or other destination.

Take a walk on stilts.

Take an extra walk around the mall when shopping for gifts and make up your own walking activities.

From *Walking Games and Activities* by June Decker and Monica Mize, 2002, Champaign, IL: Human Kinetics.

Calendar Walk Worksheet

Name: _____ **Class:** _____ **Date:** _____

Your Personal Calendar

Sunday	Monday	Tuesday	Wednesday	Thursday	Friday	Saturday

Write the walking activity that you participate in onto the calendar.

If you select a "choose your walk" day, then describe the walk you choose to do.

Initial the activities you completed.

Describe the activities you enjoyed doing the most.

How many days during the month did you participate in walking activities?

From *Walking Games and Activities* by June Decker and Monica Mize, 2002, Champaign, IL: Human Kinetics.

Card Walk

Type of Activity	Objectives	Grade Level

 Variable; 10 to 45 minutes depending on age and conditioning

Facility	Equipment	Organization
Indoor/outdoor track, gym, or other measured circular route	One or more decks of playing cards, score sheets, pencils, stopwatch, and boundary markers	Individually or in teams

Stay in designated area.

Pass on the right side.

 Explain to the students how the cards are used in the game and that you will act as the dealer.

On the go signal, students are to start walking laps around the designated area.

Each time a student passes you, hand the student a card.

After the students have completed a specific number of laps or a designated time period, have them add up the point values of the cards they collected.

The values of the cards are as follows: Aces and face cards equal 10 points each; all other cards equal the number that appears on the card.

Have students record the total value of their cards, the number of laps walked, and the distance covered on their score sheets.

The winner is the student or team with the highest score.

If the activity is done in teams, the scores of all the team members are added together, and the team with the highest score wins.

Bonus points (determined by the teacher) may be added to the individual or team that completed the most laps.

Have students answer any additional questions on the worksheet.

 The student or team with the most cards of the same suit wins.

The student or team with the most pairs or four-of-a-kind combinations wins.

The student or team with the lowest point value wins.

If a student or team receives the wildcard, they can be given five extra points or have five points taken away.

 Encourage students to walk at their best pace for greater aerobic benefits.

Example 1

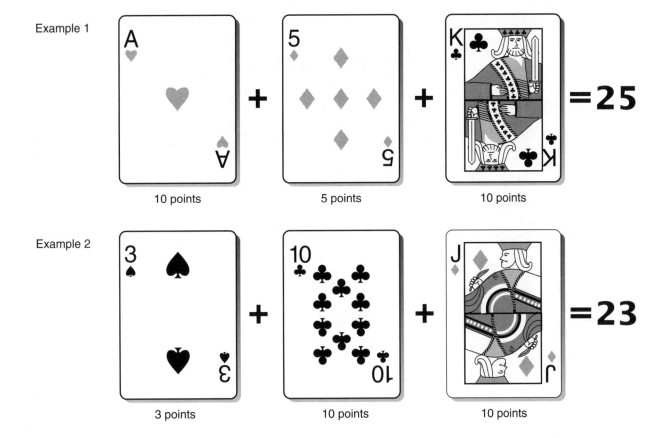

10 points   5 points   10 points

Example 2

3 points   10 points   10 points

Card Walk Worksheet

Name: _____ **Class:** _____ **Date:** _____

Please record the following information:

Names of team members	Card value	Laps completed
1.		
2.		
3.		
4.		
5.		
6.		

Total Point Value of Cards

Individual _____ *Team* _____

Total Number of Laps Walked

Individual _____ *Team* _____

Total Distance Covered

Individual _____ *Team* _____

Questions

1. What did you like about this activity and why?

2. What didn't you like about this activity and why?

3. Given the opportunity to change this game, what would you change?

From *Walking Games and Activities* by June Decker and Monica Mize, 2002, Champaign, IL: Human Kinetics.

Conversation Game

Type of Activity	Objectives	Grade Level

 From 5 to 20 minutes

Facility	Equipment	Organization
Gym or track	Pencils, worksheets	Pairs

⚠ Watch where you are going.

💡 Give students a list of specific questions to ask.

✋ Organize students into pairs.

Have students walk with their partners, interviewing each other as they go.

After students are done walking, have them record what they learned about their partners.

Have students introduce their partners to the class.

🍎 Encourage students to find out interesting things about their partners.

Conversation Game Worksheet

Name: _____ **Class:** _____ **Date:** _____

Questions

1. List five things you learned about your parnter.

2. Which of the five things did you feel was the most interesting?

3. What do you wish you had thought to ask?

From *Walking Games and Activities* by June Decker and Monica Mize, 2002, Champaign, IL: Human Kinetics.

WALKING GAMES AND ACTIVITIES

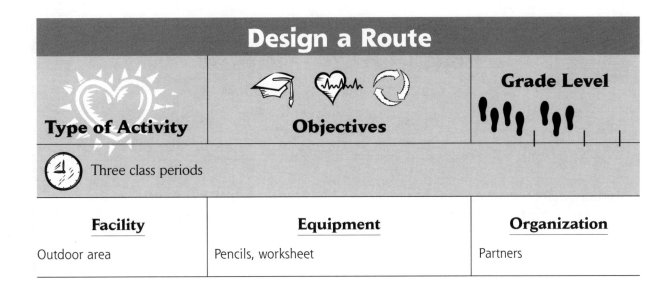

Design a Route

Type of Activity	Objectives	Grade Level
Three class periods		

Facility	Equipment	Organization
Outdoor area	Pencils, worksheet	Partners

Prerequisite Mini-lecture

Choosing a Route

Watch where you are going.

Stay in designated area.

Give each student a pencil and a worksheet.

Have students select a partner for whom they will design a route.

Instruct students to walk, creating a route for their partner. Remind students of the criteria for a good route.

Identify areas in which students can walk when designing their route (e.g., around the school building, parking lot, track, and playing field).

Choose ample sites so students have a challenging workout.

Do not allow students to disrupt normal school functions as they design their route.

On day 2, the student for whom the route was designed walks it as quickly as possible. Record the time for each student.

On day 3, the student who designed the route walks it as quickly as possible. The idea is to beat the partner's time of the previous day. Again, record the time.

The partner who walks the route the fastest is the winner.

Students may work in pairs to design a route for another pair.

Design a Route Worksheet

Name: _____ **Class:** _____ **Date:** _____

Design a walking route for your partner to follow. The route should take your partner most of the class period to complete. List each turn your partner should take. For example:

Begin at College and D
Take D to 8th
Go left on 8th to Cooper

Record the time it took to complete the route.

Route designer:

Time:

Route recipient:

Time:

From *Walking Games and Activities* by June Decker and Monica Mize, 2002, Champaign, IL: Human Kinetics.

Destination Walk

Type of Activity 	Objectives	Grade Level 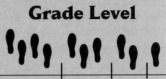

 From 5 to 15 minutes (This activity takes place over several class periods.)

Facility	Equipment	Organization
Outdoor or indoor track, gymnasium, or playing field	Pencil and score sheet per student, stopwatch, and boundary markers	Individuals, partners, teams, or entire class

Walk in designated area or route.

Be aware of other walkers.

Designate a time period at the beginning of each class for students to accumulate miles (kilometers).

Determine the area for the walking activity to take place.

Have students select a destination (post office, grocery store, nearby town, next state or province) and determine the number of miles (kilometers) to the destination from school.

Have students set their goal for the time it will take to reach their destination.

Determine the date the activity will begin.

Distribute score sheets to students and explain how to record information on the score sheets.

Have students do the activity with a partner.

Have students do the activity in teams.

Have students do the activity as a class-against-class competition.

Designate a specific number of days to reach a common goal and have students determine how they will achieve that goal.

Have a party if the students reach their destination. Make the party activity relate to the destination. For example, if the destination was New Orleans, the students could earn Mardi gras beads; if the destination was Chicago, they could earn a Chicago hot dog or pizza; if the destination was New York City, they could earn a big apple; and if the destination was Salt Lake City, they could earn saltwater taffy.

 Determine the number of days students will do the destination walk so that they can set realistic goals. Take into account that students are only walking for a short period on any given day.

Destination Walk Worksheet

Name: _____ **Class:** _____ **Date:** _____

Destination: _____
Miles (kilometers) to destination: _____

Day	Distance goal	Actual miles (kilometers) walked	Total miles (kilometers) to date	Comments
1				
2				
3				
4				
5				
6				
7				
8				
9				
10				
11				
12				
13				
14				
15				
16				
17				
18				
19				
20				

Total miles (kilometers) walked: _____

From *Walking Games and Activities* by June Decker and Monica Mize, 2002, Champaign, IL: Human Kinetics.

(continued)

(continued)

Questions

1. Did you reach your destination?

2. Did you reach your time goal?

3. If you did not reach your goal, how close did you come?

4. Did you enjoy the activity? Why or why not?

5. Other comments about the activity:

From *Walking Games and Activities* by June Decker and Monica Mize, 2002, Champaign, IL: Human Kinetics.

Double Your Fun

Type of Activity	Objectives	Grade Level

🕐 Entire class period

Facility	Equipment	Organization
Indoor/outdoor track, gym, or other measured circular route	Pencils, score sheet, and stopwatch for each student; boundary markers	Individual

Prerequisite Mini-lectures

Taking Your Pulse

Calculating Your Target Heart Rate

 Walk in designated area and be aware of other walkers.

Pass on the right side only.

 Pass out equipment to students.

Have students record resting heart rate and target heart rate range on the score sheet.

Instruct students to walk around the designated area and, after completing two laps, have them take their heart rate and record it on the score sheet.

Have students repeat this sequence for a designated time period. At the end of the time period, have them record the additional information indicated on the score sheet.

Double Your Fun Worksheet

Name: _____ **Class:** _____ **Date:** _____

Please record all necessary information on the score sheet:

Resting heart rate: _____

Target heart rates: _____ 60 percent _____ 90 percent

Record heart rate after every two laps.

1.

2.

3.

4.

5.

6.

7.

8.

9.

10.

From *Walking Games and Activities* by June Decker and Monica Mize, 2002, Champaign, IL: Human Kinetics.

Total laps walked: _____

Distance covered: _____

Duration of walk: _____

Number of laps walked in target zone: _____

Question

1. Based on the results, would you need to change the activity to make it aerobically beneficial? If so, how would you change it?

Estimated Pace

Type of Activity	Objectives	Grade Level

 Variable depending on distance walked, age, and conditioning

Facility	Equipment	Organization
Indoor/outdoor track, gym, or other measured circular route	Stopwatch, pencil, and worksheet per student (If one stopwatch per student is not available, students can work with a partner or in small groups and time each other.)	Individual race against self

 Stay on designated route.

Be aware of others around you.

 Have students start watches and leave them with the instructor so that they cannot see their time as they walk.

Do not allow students to have timing devices with them during the activity.

 Have students estimate their times for the half-mile, mile, mile-and-a-half, and two-mile (or comparable metric distances such as 800, 1,500, or 3,000 meters) distances and write them on the worksheet.

Have students walk and time their walk.

Have students record their actual times on the worksheet

Have students write their personal comments about the activity.

Estimated Pace Worksheet

Name: _____ **Class:** _____ **Date:** _____

What is your estimated time for walking the following distances?

1/2 mile (.8 kilometer): _____

1 mile (1.6 kilometers): _____

1-1/2 miles (2.4 kilometers): _____

2 miles (3.2 kilometers): _____

What was your actual time for walking the same distances as above?

1/2 mile (.8 kilometer): _____

1 mile (1.6 kilometers): _____

1-1/2 miles (2.4 kilometers): _____

2 miles (3.2 kilometers): _____

Were you faster or slower than you estimated?

Comments:

From *Walking Games and Activities* by June Decker and Monica Mize, 2002, Champaign, IL: Human Kinetics.

15-Minute Paper Clip Walk

Type of Activity

Objectives

Grade Level

 Fifteen minutes

Facility	Equipment	Organization
Indoor/outdoor track, gym, or other measured circular route	Two or three boxes of paper clips, boundary markers, stopwatch, pencil, and score sheet	Individual

Prerequisite Mini-lectures

Taking Your Pulse

Calculating Your Target Heart Rate

 Walk in designated area and pass on the right side.

Do not interfere with other walkers.

Encourage students to walk as fast as they can.

Have all students begin walking at the same time from the starting line.

Each time the students complete a lap, give them a paper clip to help them keep track of their laps.

At the 15-minute point, blow the whistle and instruct the students to freeze where they are and find their pulse.

Blow the whistle a second time and have the students start counting their pulse.

When you blow the whistle the third time, the students are to stop counting their pulse and write their heart rate on the score sheet, multiplying it by 10.

Repeat the activity for another 15-minute period.

At the end of the activity, have students record their paper clip count. The student with the most paper clips wins.

Do the activity for a different amount of time.

Have students determine if their heart rate reached their target heart rate zone. Students whose heart rate reaches their target zone could receive one bonus point.

Group students into small teams. Have them add each team member's total laps together to determine a team score. You could also give a bonus point to each team member whose heart rate reached their target zone.

 Encourage students to walk at their best pace to keep the game moving and to help identify individual walking speeds.

15-Minute Paper Clip Walk Worksheet

Name: _____ **Class:** _____ **Date:** _____

Please record all information on the score sheet.

Walking heart rate: _____ × 10 = _____

Paper clip score: _____

Fraction of the last lap that was completed: _____

Your paper clip walking score is the number of laps completed plus your position on the course at the final whistle. _____

Did you reach your target heart rate? _____

Find a Friend

Type of Activity	Objectives	Grade Level

 From 15 to 30 minutes

Facility	Equipment	Organization
Indoor/outdoor track, gym, or other measured circular route	Worksheets, pencils	Rotating pairs

⚠️ Watch where you are going.

🍎 The more friends the students have to find, the more fun the game is.

☞ Have students begin walking around the area.

Instruct students that when you call out, "Find a friend," they are to partner with the person walking closest to them.

Tell students to discuss their favorite animal with their partner.

When you tell them to find a friend again, students are to find a new partner and discuss their favorite videos.

Repeat this process with new topics for as long as you wish.

Then instruct students to walk solo again as you randomly call out the topics—book, video, animal, and so on. Students are to find the person with whom they discussed each topic called. Call topics quickly so students must hurry to move from partner to partner.

Find a Friend Worksheet

Name: _____ **Class:** _____ **Date:** _____

1. Who was your book friend?

2. Who was your animal friend?

3. Who was your video friend?

4. Who was your song friend?

5. Who was your class friend?

6. Who was your sport friend?

7. Who was your clothes friend?

8. Who was your song friend?

9. Who was your restaurant friend?

10. Who was your car friend?

From *Walking Games and Activities* by June Decker and Monica Mize, 2002, Champaign, IL: Human Kinetics.

Grab Bag Workout

Type of Activity	Objectives	Grade Level

 From 15 to 30 minutes

Facility	Equipment	Organization
Indoor/outdoor track, gym, or other measured circular route	Dependent on each student's route (Students are given a list of areas and equipment that they can use on their route.) Pencil, worksheet	Dependent on each student's route and will be included in the description of the activity

 Follow the directions of your route.

Stay in designated area.

Be aware of other walkers.

 Instruct students to design a walking route using the facilities available (track, stairs, bikes, jump rope, walking poles, weight machine, exercise area). For this type of route, divide students into groups and have them walk the route as a circuit, with each group beginning the route at a different facility.

The route must last for 15 to 30 minutes.

Students must identify the objectives of the activities they design.

All students put their routes into a box and each student draws one route from the box. If students draw their own route, they must return it to the box and draw another.

Each student completes the route that is drawn from the box.

 Students could participate in this activity as teams. For instance, one member of the team could draw a grab bag activity from the box and the entire team do that activity.

 Have students select at least three of the activity options listed above. Encourage students to be creative in developing their own route. For example, students could walk two laps around the track using the walking poles. At the end of the two laps, they could jump rope for one minute. After jumping rope, they could walk up and down the stairs twice.

Grab Bag Workout Worksheet 1

Name: _____ **Class:** _____ **Date:** _____

Length of activity:

Objectives of activity:

Equipment needed:

Description of the routine:

From *Walking Games and Activities* by June Decker and Monica Mize, 2002, Champaign, IL: Human Kinetics.

Grab Bag Workout Worksheet 2

Name: _____ **Class:** _____ **Date:** _____

Write an evaluation of the workout routine. Describe how you felt about the routine in terms of variety of activities, originality, difficulty, ease of understanding directions, duration of workout, and enjoyment and benefits of workout.

Hot Pursuit

Type of Activity	Objectives	Grade Level
(clock icon) Entire class period		

Facility	Equipment	Organization
Any walking route	Worksheet, route map, pencils	Pairs

 Walk within your target heart rate range.

 Divide class into pairs of approximately equal ability.

Have pairs line up in order of speed from slowest to fastest.

Have the slowest pair start first, followed by the second slowest pair, and so on, with the fastest pair starting last.

Each pair should try to pass as many other pairs as possible without being caught from behind.

Pairs must stay together and follow the established route.

No running is allowed.

Hot Pursuit Worksheet

Name: _____ **Class:** _____ **Date:** _____

Questions

1. Did you walk faster or slower than you usually do? Why?

2. What made this game difficult?

3. How would you change this game if you could?

From *Walking Games and Activities* by June Decker and Monica Mize, 2002, Champaign, IL: Human Kinetics.

M&M Terminator

Type of Activity	Objectives	Grade Level
Entire class period		The activity must be adjusted to meet the developmental levels of the students participating in the game.

Facility	Equipment	Organization
Indoor/outdoor track, gym, or other measured circular route	M&Ms, score sheet, and pencil for each student	Individual

Prerequisite Mini-lecture

Caloric Expenditure

Be aware of other walkers.

Pass on the right side only.

Distribute M&Ms, pencils, and score sheets to students.

Tell students how many calories are in the M&Ms (five calories per regular-sized M&M).

Tell students that they burn about 100 calories per mile (62 per kilometer).

Tells students the distance of the track or specified route.

Have students determine how many M&Ms they can burn in 30 minutes if they burn 25 calories per quarter mile (15.5 per quarter kilometer).

Repeat the activity using different types of food.

If some elementary students are unable to do the calculations, have them walk a certain number of laps, then give them the number of M&Ms burned in walking that distance.

M&M Terminator Worksheet

Name: **Class:**   **Date:**

Distance walked:

Calories burned:

Number of M&Ms burned:

Generally, you burn approximately 100 calories per mile of walking (62 per kilometer). Based on the distance you walked, which of the following foods could you have burned off?

1 M&M—5 calories

Half of a bagel—76 calories

12-ounce soda—161 calories

Macaroni with cheese, 1 cup—464 calories

Popcorn, 1 cup—54 calories

Yogurt, 1 cup—150 calories

Cookie, 1 plain—75 calories

1 doughnut—250 calories

1 banana—88 calories

1 orange—60 calories

1 hamburger—350 calories

1 boiled egg—77 calories

Cooked broccoli, 1 cup—60 calories

1 slice of cheese pizza—376 calories

half of a bagel

yogurt

orange

12-ounce soda

doughnut

macaroni with cheese

hamburger

candy

boiled egg

popcorn

cookie

cheeze pizza

banana

cooked broccoli

From *Walking Games and Activities* by June Decker and Monica Mize, 2002, Champaign, IL: Human Kinetics.

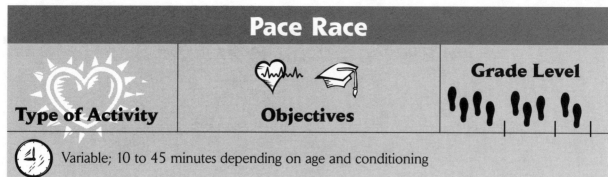

Pace Race

Type of Activity	Objectives	Grade Level

 Variable; 10 to 45 minutes depending on age and conditioning

Facility	Equipment	Organization
Any measured route	Stopwatch, pencil, worksheet per student	Individual race against self

Prerequisite Mini-lectures

Taking Your Pulse
Calculating Your Target Heart Rate

 Have students place watches in a plastic bag that you keep with you at all times.

 Stay on designated route.

Be aware of other students on the route.

 Identify a walking route for students.

Have students write their estimated time for walking a specific route on the worksheet.

Do not allow students to have any timing devices with them during the activity.

Have students record their actual finishing time on the worksheet.

The person finishing closest to their estimated time is the winner of that day's activity.

Have students finish filling out the worksheet.

No running is allowed.

Pace Race Worksheet

Name: _____ **Class:** _____ **Date:** _____

Resting heart rate: _____

Target heart rates: _____ 60 percent _____ 90 percent

Distance to be walked: _____

Estimated time to complete the race: _____

Actual race time: _____

Ending heart rate: _____

Did you reach your target zone? _____

Difference in time between estimated time and actual time completing the race: _____

Questions

1. Did you come as close as you expected? Why or why not?

2. Did you enjoy this activity? Why or why not?

From *Walking Games and Activities* by June Decker and Monica Mize, 2002, Champaign, IL: Human Kinetics.

Pass Back and Walk Forward

Type of Activity 	Objectives	Grade Level
Determined by instructor		

Facility	Equipment	Organization
Gymnasium or track	One stuffed animal (or other object), pencil, and worksheet per group	Gruops of five to eight in a line, one behind the other

 Pass only on the right side.

Be aware of other groups.

 Organize students into groups of five to eight depending on class size.

Have students form a line, one behind the other, all facing the same direction.

The first person in the line carries an object.

The group starts walking, with the person in front setting the pace.

As the students walk forward in their group, the first person in line hands the object back to the next, and this continues until the object has reached the last person in the line.

When the last person in the line receives the object, that person walks as fast as they can to the front of the line, and the sequence is repeated.

Have the group continue repeating the sequence for a specified time or distance (i.e., 5 minutes, 10 minutes, half mile, mile, 500 meters, 1,000 meters).

The activity is complete when the students are back in the same order they were in at the start or have walked for the specified amount of time or distance.

Time the activity; the group finishing with the fastest time wins.

 Change members of the group to keep the ability level better distributed.

Match the stuffed animal or object being passed with the time of year (e.g., a stuffed pumpkin around Halloween or a stuffed turkey around Thanksgiving; the game could then be renamed Pass the Pumpkin or Pass the Turkey).

 Encourage students to get through as many complete rotations as possible.

Pass Back and Walk Forward Worksheet

Name: _____   **Class:** _____   **Date:** _____

Names of group members:

Time for one complete sequence (the time from when the group members start passing back the object until they return to their initial starting order): _____

Number of sequences needed to complete 1/2 mile (.8 kilometer): _____ 1 mile (1.6 kilometers): _____

Time to complete 1/2 mile (.8 kilometer): _____ 1 mile (1.6 kilometers): _____

Questions

1. How could you work with your group to improve your sequence time?

2. How would you improve this game?

From *Walking Games and Activities* by June Decker and Monica Mize, 2002, Champaign, IL: Human Kinetics.

Stair Route

Type of Activity	Objective	Grade Level

  From 20 to 30 minutes

Facility	Equipment	Organization
Flight of stairs combined with walking area (e.g., gymnasium bleachers and floor or track and stadium stairs)	Score sheet, pencil, stop watch	Individual

Prerequisite Mini-lectures

Taking your Pulse
Calculating Your Target Heart Rate

Make sure students walk up and down the stairs rather than jog.

 Walk up and down stairs on the right.

Be aware of other walkers.

Walk, do not run, down the stairs.

 Have students walk one lap around the designated area and make one trip up and down the stairs. Repeat this sequence as many times as possible in the time allotted.

At the end of each five-minute period, have students record the number of laps completed and their heart rate.

At the end of the allotted time, have students complete the additional information on the worksheet.

Stair Route Worksheet

Name: _____ **Class:** _____ **Date:** _____

Record resting heart rate: _____

Record target heart rates: _____ 60 percent _____ 90 percent

Number of laps	*Heart rate*
5 minutes	
10 minutes	
15 minutes	
20 minutes	

Questions

1. How many minutes did you work with your heart rate in the target zone?

2. Did you get your heart rate above your 90 percent limit?

3. Comments about the activity?

4. Did stairs affect your heart rate more than level ground?

5. Did you like this activity more or less than a regular route?

6. How would you improve the activity?

From *Walking Games and Activities* by June Decker and Monica Mize, 2002, Champaign, IL: Human Kinetics.

Touchdown Walk

Type of Activity

Objectives

Grade Level

 Entire class period

Facility	Equipment	Organization
Football field or measured area	Pencil and score sheet per student, boundary markers, and stopwatch	Individual

 Watch where you are going.

Be aware of other walkers.

 Divide class into teams and make it competitive among the teams.

Game can be played on a soccer field and scored as soccer goals.

Game can be played on a basketball court and scored as field goals.

This activity can be played by quarters, halves, or for an entire game. Determine the length of the playing period (e.g., quarters of 4, 5, 6, or 7 minutes).

Have students walk as many trips up and down the football field as possible in the specified time period (walk goal line to goal line). Each time students walk from goal line to goal line, they score a touchdown.

Have students record the number of touchdowns scored on their score sheet.

 Put students on teams, have them choose their favorite university or professional team, and run the activity as a tournament.

Touchdown Walk Worksheet

Name: _____ **Class:** _____ **Date:** _____

Individual   *Touchdowns per quarter*

Team:	*1st*	*2nd*	*3rd*	*4th*	*Total*	*Distance covered*

Team total   *Touchdowns per quarter*

Team:	*1st*	*2nd*	*3rd*	*4th*	*Total*	*Distance covered*

From *Walking Games and Activities* by June Decker and Monica Mize, 2002, Champaign, IL: Human Kinetics.

Tour de France Walking Race

Type of Activity	Objectives	Grade Level 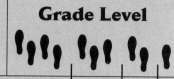

 Variable depending on distance selected

Facility	Equipment	Organization
Indoor or outdoor track, gymnasium, or any measured route	Jersey or T-shirt, stopwatch	Individual

 Walk within the boundaries.

Be aware of other walkers.

Describe the tradition of the Tour de France in which the current leader gets to wear the yellow jersey.

You can design the walk to be a mile, a mile and a half, two miles (or comparable metric distances such as 1,500, 2,000, or 3,000 meters), or any distance you select.

You can vary the distance each time.

Randomly select a student to be the winner of the previous race and have the honor of wearing the winning T-shirt.

Have all participants begin the activity together on the go signal and walk around the designated area for a specified time or distance.

At the end of the walk, the previous winner is awarded five points for each walker he or she beats, and each student who beats the walker in the T-shirt receives three points.

Add up the points to determine if the walker with the T-shirt continues his or her winning streak.

If the current winner does not continue to win, then randomly select a student from those beating the current winner.

If desired, you can limit the number of times one person can continue to win.

Example

Previous winner beats four walkers = 20 points

Nine students beat the walker in the T-shirt = 27 points

Therefore, a new walker would then be chosen as the race winner and a new race would begin.

 Vary the walking route so students do not get into a routine.

Tour de France Walking Race Worksheet

Name: _____ **Class:** _____ **Date:** _____

Questions

1. Tour de France involves an aerobic activity different from walking. What is that?

2. How are the Tour de France Walk Race and the real Tour de France alike and/or different?

3. How can you work together in this game to help take over the winning position?

From *Walking Games and Activities* by June Decker and Monica Mize, 2002, Champaign, IL: Human Kinetics.

Walk Aerobics

Type of Activity	Objectives	Grade Level

🕐 Entire class period

Facility	Equipment	Organization
Gymnasium, multipurpose room, or any other open area or field	Tape or CD player, music of choice	Lines

Watch where you are going.

Be aware of others around you.

Explain the term aerobic to the class. (Aerobic: The longer and harder one participates, the more oxygen that is needed.)

Explain the term aerobic endurance to the class. (Aerobic endurance: The heart and lungs are doing a good job of sending oxygen to the muscles so one can exercise for long time periods.)

Teach the aerobic routine in a progressive manner:

1. Explain and demonstrate steps.

2. Practice steps 1, 2, 3, and 4.

3. Put steps 1, 2, 3, and 4 to music.

4. Repeat with steps 5, 6, 7, and 8.

5. Add steps 1, 2, 3, 4, 5, 6, 7, and 8 together; practice without music, then with music.

6. Continue until all steps have been covered.

Divide students into groups of five or six, depending on class size.

Provide each group with some music.

Have each group design its own aerobic routine.

Each routine must include a minimum of eight different patterns of steps. Each pattern is done for eight counts. (Example: Walk forward for eight counts, walk backward for eight counts. That represents two different patterns.)

These steps can be repeated.

Have each group teach its routine to the class.

In groups or individually, have students design their own aerobic workout.

Use music that students enjoy.

Walk Aerobics Routine

Walk in place for eight counts

Walk to the left for eight counts

Walk to the right for eight counts

Walk in place for eight counts

Walk forward for eight counts

Walk backward for eight counts

Walk in place for eight counts

Walk on the heels forward for eight counts

Walk backward for eight counts

Walk in place for eight counts

Walk on the toes forward for eight counts

Walk backward for eight counts

Walk in place for eight counts

Duck walk forward for eight counts

Walk backward for eight counts

Walk pigeon-toed forward for eight counts

Walk backward for eight counts

Walk in place for eight counts

Walk to the left with a grapevine step for eight counts

Walk to the right with a grapevine step for eight counts

Walk in place for eight counts

Variety Walks

Heel walk: walk with a pronounced heel-toe stride (emphasis on shins)

Toe walk: walk on balls of feet (emphasis on calves)

Duck walk: turn feet and knees outward (emphasis on hips and outer thighs)

Pigeon-toed walk: turn feet and knees inward (emphasis on hips and inner thighs)

Grapevine: step right, left over right, step right, step left behind right, front, side, back, side, together

Walk Aerobics Worksheet

Name: _____   **Class:** _____   **Date:** _____

With your group, design your own walk aerobic routine. Include a minimum of eight different patterns of steps, with each pattern done for eight counts. (Example: Walk forward for eight counts, walk backward for eight counts. That represents two different patterns.) You may repeat steps. Now teach your group's routine to the class.

Names of Group Members _____

Describe walk aerobics routine in the spaces below:

8 counts:

8 counts:

8 counts:

8 counts:

8 counts:

8 counts:

8 counts:

8 counts:

Repeat

Questions

1. If you had to design another walk aerobic routine, what would you do differently?

2. What patterns would you retain?

3. What did you learn from this activity?

From *Walking Games and Activities* by June Decker and Monica Mize, 2002, Champaign, IL: Human Kinetics.

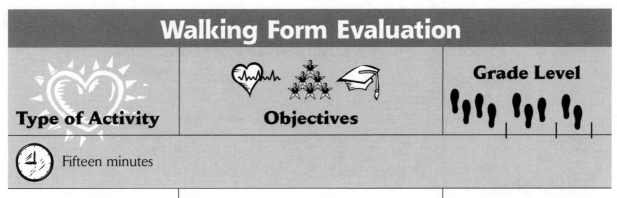

Walking Form Evaluation

Type of Activity	Objectives	Grade Level

🕐 Fifteen minutes

Facility	Equipment	Organization
Indoor/outdoor track, gym, or other measured circular route	One worksheet and one pen/pencil per student	Pairs

Prerequisite Mini-lecture

Learning Proper Techniques

 Be aware of other students in the class.

 Demonstrate proper walking form and go over the evaluation form before starting so students know what to look for.

Have students self-evaluate their walking form, including filling out the self-assessment checklist based on how well they think they walked.

Next, have students pair off. One student is to walk while the other student assesses their walking form, and then they are to reverse roles.

Have students compare their self-assessment with their partner's assessment of them.

Have students answer the questions on the worksheet.

Walking Form Evaluation Worksheet

Name: _____ **Class:** _____ **Date:** _____

Self-Checklist

Place a check by the parts of the walking form you think you are doing correctly.

_____ Back straight

_____ 45-degree heel strike

_____ Shoulders over hips

_____ Push off toes

_____ Head up

_____ Arms swing

_____ Toes straight

Instructions

Walk with a partner, observing them from the back and from the side. Put a check mark beside the parts of the walking form your partner is doing correctly.

Walker: _____ *Evaluator:* _____

_____ Back straight

_____ 45-degree heel strike

_____ Shoulders over hips

_____ Pushes off toes

_____ Head up

_____ Arms swing

_____ Toes straight

Questions

1. What were the differences between the way your partner evaluated your walking form and how you thought you walked?

2. What parts of your walking form do you need to improve?

From *Walking Games and Activities* by June Decker and Monica Mize, 2002, Champaign, IL: Human Kinetics.

Who's My Partner?

Type of Activity	Objective	Grade Level

Variable; 10 or more minutes

Facility	Equipment	Organization
Track or gym	Index cards, pairs of numbers	Individual

Don't run into anyone else.

Have students walk fast laps around the designated area for the allotted time.

After walking, have students record the number of laps (to the nearest quarter lap) completed.

Have students draw numbers. Students who draw matching numbers are partners.

Have partners add their total number of laps together.

The pair with the highest total number of laps is the winner.

For variety, have students change directions often. This also helps them with adding fractions or decimals.

Who's My Partner? Worksheet

Name: _____   **Class:** _____   **Date:** _____

Questions

1. Did you walk as fast as you can today?

2. Did you like not knowing who your partner was? Why?

3. Would you have walked faster or slower if you knew who your partner was? Why?

4. How would you change this game?

From *Walking Games and Activities* by June Decker and Monica Mize, 2002, Champaign, IL: Human Kinetics.

Beat That Lap

Type of Activity

Objectives

Grade Level

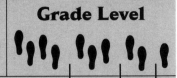

 Variable; 10 to 45 minutes depending on age and conditioning

Facility	Equipment	Organization
Track, gymnasium	If one stopwatch per student is not available, students can work in pairs or small groups and can time each other.	Individual

Prerequisite Mini-lectures

Taking Your Pulse
Calculating Your Target Heart Rate

 Stay in designated area.

Be aware of other walkers.

 Have students record name, resting heart rate, and target heart rate range onto worksheet.

Have students time their first lap around the track and write the time on the score sheet.

Have students reset stopwatch and time the second lap, trying to beat the time on lap 1.

Record the time on the worksheet.

Have students repeat this process on lap 3, trying to beat that time on lap 4, and again on lap 5, trying to beat that time on lap 6, and so on, for the time period designated.

Answer questions on the worksheet relating to your workout.

💡 Choose the total number of laps to be walked based on current fitness level and length of walking track.

 Make sure students know how to work stopwatches before beginning activity.

Beat That Lap Worksheet

Name: _____ **Class:** _____ **Date:** _____

Please provide the following information and answers to the questions. Record lap times in seconds.

Resting heart rate: _____

Target heart rates: _____ 60 percent _____ 90 percent

Time of 1st lap: _____

Time of 2nd lap: _____

Did you beat the time on your 1st lap? _____

If yes, by how much? _____

Time of 3rd lap: _____

Time of 4th lap: _____

Did you beat the time on your 3rd lap? _____

If yes, by how much? _____

Time of 5th lap: _____

Time of 6th lap: _____

Did you beat the time on your 5th lap? _____

If yes, by how much? _____

Take your heart rate and record it. _____

Are you in your target zone? _____

Time of 7th lap: _____

Time of 8th lap: _____

Did you beat the time on your 7th lap? _____

If yes, by how much? _____

Time of 9th lap: _____

Time of 10th lap: _____

Did you beat the time on your 9th lap? _____

If yes, by how much? _____

Take your heart rate and record it. _____

Are you in your target zone? _____

From *Walking Games and Activities* by June Decker and Monica Mize, 2002, Champaign, IL: Human Kinetics.

Questions

1. How many times were you able to "beat that lap"? _____

2. Which lap did you have the fastest time on? _____

3. Record the total number of laps walked. _____

4. Did you enjoy the activity? Why or why not?

5. What did you learn from this activity?

6. Other comments:

From *Walking Games and Activities* by June Decker and Monica Mize, 2002, Champaign, IL: Human Kinetics.

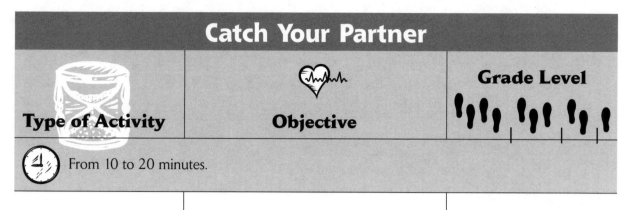

Catch Your Partner

Type of Activity	Objective	Grade Level

🕐 From 10 to 20 minutes.

Facility	Equipment	Organization
Track or gym	Pencil and worksheet per student	Pairs

 Don't run into anyone else.

 Organize students in pairs.

Have students decide who is partner 1 ① and who is partner 2 ②.

All students designated as partner 2 are to go directly across the track or gym from partner 1.

On the given signal, all students designated as partner 2 (2a) are to begin walking slowly around the area while students designated as partner 1 (1a) begin walking as fast as possible in pursuit.

When partner 1 (1b) catches partner 2 (2b), the roles are reversed, with students designated as partner 1 (1c) walking slowly while those designated as partner 2 (2c) try to catch them.

No running is allowed.

Remind slow walkers not to speed up, if necessary.

 You can make this activity more interesting by having all walkers reverse direction on your signal.

 Have students change direction often to keep the game lively.

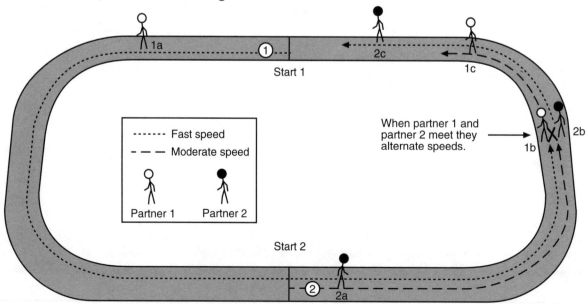

Start 1

Start 2

- - - - - Fast speed

– – – Moderate speed

Partner 1   Partner 2

When partner 1 and partner 2 meet they alternate speeds.

Catch Your Partner Worksheet

Name: _____ **Class:** _____ **Date:** _____

Questions

1. How did you walk differently when walking fast and walking slow?

2. What made going fast difficult?

3. What made going slow difficult?

Cowpokes and Rustlers

  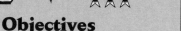

Type of Activity	Objectives	Grade Level
Entire class period		

Facility	Equipment	Organization
Large indoor or outdoor space with two corrals marked by cones	Jerseys, pencils, worksheets	Individuals

 Use gentle tags.

Using cones, create two large corrals some distance apart (e.g., one at each end of the football field).

Divide class into three groups: two students are cowpokes, two are rustlers, and the rest are cattle.

The object of the game for the cowpokes and rustlers is to catch and keep as many cattle as possible. The object of the game for the cattle is to avoid getting caught or escape if caught.

Give jerseys of one color to the cowpokes and another color to the rustlers.

Assign one corral to the cowpokes and the other to the rustlers.

Have the cattle begin walking. After one minute, the cowpokes are to begin trying to catch as many cattle as possible.

When cattle are tagged, they are taken to the corral belonging to the tagger. They must continue walking after they are put in the corral.

Cattle who haven't been caught can enter the corral and free those penned inside.

Cowpokes can steal cattle from the rustlers' corral by tagging those in the pen and taking them to the

cowpokes' corral. Rustlers can also steal cattle from the cowpokes.

After a few minutes of play, count the cattle in each pen, have students change roles, and play again.

No running is allowed.

Upon completion of the game, have students complete the accompanying worksheet.

 For large classes, have students work in pairs rather than individually.

 Tell students that if they develop a plan and work together with others in their group, they will be more successful.

Cowpokes'
corral

Rustlers'
corral

○	cowpoke (2)
●	rustler (2)
●	cattle

Cowpokes and Rustlers Worksheet

Name: **Class:**   **Date:**

Questions

1. Which job (cowpoke, rustler, cattle) did you like the best? Why?

2. How well did you work with others in your group?

3. What could groups have done to be more successful?

4. How would you change this game if you could?

From *Walking Games and Activities* by June Decker and Monica Mize, 2002, Champaign, IL: Human Kinetics.

Coyotes and Roadrunners

Type of Activity	Objectives	Grade Level
		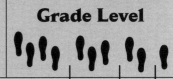

 Variable; 10 to 45 minutes depending on age and conditioning

Facility	Equipment	Organization
Indoor or outdoor track, gym, or other measured circular route	Boundary markers, two or three sets of jerseys, pencil and worksheet per student	Pairs

   Stay in designated area.

Follow rules.

Use gentle tags.

   Organize students into pairs.

Designate two or three pairs (depending on number of students) as coyotes.

Give jerseys to coyotes.

Identify remaining students as roadrunners.

Give roadrunners a two-minute head start within the designated area.

After two minutes, have coyotes start walking, trying to catch the roadrunners.

If a roadrunner pair is caught, they become coyotes and the coyotes become roadrunners.

No tag-backs are allowed.

Partners must stay together.

No running is allowed.

Do not allow students to hide to keep from being caught. Everyone must keep walking at all times.

Coyotes and Roadrunners Worksheet

Name: _____ **Class:** _____ **Date:** _____

Questions

1. What did you like about this game?

2. What didn't you like about this game?

3. How would you change this game?

4. Which did you like being the most: a coyote or a roadrunner? Why?

From *Walking Games and Activities* by June Decker and Monica Mize, 2002, Champaign, IL: Human Kinetics.

Discover Your School

 Type of Activity	 Objectives	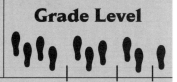 Grade Level
Entire class period		

Facility	Equipment	Organization
Indoors or outdoors on campus	Game sheets, pencils, letter cards, and worksheets	Pairs or groups of three

 Stay in designated area.

 Using 3 x 5 index cards cut in half, make letter cards that, when combined, spell words that make a sentence.

Place the letter cards in appropriate places on campus.

Make worksheets.

Divide the class into groups of two or three.

Instruct students to walk to each site on the worksheets and record the letter they find there.

No information should be shared with any other group.

When a group has found all the letters, it returns to the starting point and unscrambles the letters to make a sentence.

The team that returns and solves the problem first is the winner.

Team members must stay together, and no running is allowed.

 Choose sites on campus that are interesting and not frequently visited by most students. Remind students to be respectful and not disrupt other classes or events as they "discover their school."

Discover Your School Sample Clues

Name of team members:	Class:	Date:

Location	Letter
Computer Lab	I
Student Activity Office	W
Dr. Mize's Office	L
Wellness Center	F
Science Building	F
McCray Gallery	T
Hunter Hall	G
Library-Treasure Room	A
Dr. Otte's Office	S
Preschool	K
Museum	I
Learning Resource Center	N
Softball Field	A
Light Hall Elevator	N
School of Education Office	U
Purchasing Office	!
Dr. Decker's Office	S

Solution: Walking fast is fun!

From *Walking Games and Activities* by June Decker and Monica Mize, 2002, Champaign, IL: Human Kinetics.

Discover Your School Clues Team Worksheet

Name of team members: **Class:**   **Date:**

Location	Letter
1.	_____
2.	_____
3.	_____
4.	_____
5.	_____
6.	_____
7.	_____
8.	_____
9.	_____
10.	_____
11.	_____
12.	_____
13.	_____
14.	_____
15.	_____
16.	_____
17.	_____

Solution:

From *Walking Games and Activities* by June Decker and Monica Mize, 2002, Champaign, IL: Human Kinetics.

Find a Corner

Type of Activity	Objectives	Grade Level
 Entire class period		

Facility	Equipment	Organization
Outdoor area	Pencils, Find a Corner clues sheets, and worksheets	Pairs or groups of three

 Stay in designated area.

 Divide students into pairs or teams of three.

Give each group a Find a Corner clues sheet (see Sample Clues Sheet, page 121).

Have students walk to the corners indicated and record where they are when they get there. No corner may be used twice; however, the same street may be used twice.

All group members must stay together.

No running is allowed.

Students may select the order in which they find the corners.

 If you wish to keep your students on campus, you can use building corners or sidewalk corners instead of street corners.

 Choose ample sites so students will have a challenging workout.

Find a Corner Sample Clues

Walk to the appropriate corner and record where you are.

At the top of a hill

With a church

With a school

Where one street is named for a color and one is a number

Where one street is named for a southern state

Where one street is named for a state capital

With a government building

With a fast-food restaurant

With a sit-down restaurant

Where one street has a two-word Spanish name

Where one street is named for the state immediately west of New Mexico

Where one street is named for the state immediately east of New Mexico

Where one street is named for the home of the 1849 Gold Rush

That is downtown

Where one street is named for an educational institution

From *Walking Games and Activities* by June Decker and Monica Mize, 2002, Champaign, IL: Human Kinetics.

Find a Corner Team Worksheet

Walk to the appropriate corner and record where you are.

1.

2.

3.

4.

5.

6.

7.

8.

9.

10.

11.

12.

13.

14.

15.

Questions

1. If you were to do this activity again tomorrow, what different strategies would you use to find your corners faster?

2. Describe how well you and your partner(s) worked together.

3. What suggestions do you have for changing this game?

From *Walking Games and Activities* by June Decker and Monica Mize, 2002, Champaign, IL: Human Kinetics.

Mad Scramble

Type of Activity	Objectives	Grade Level
🕐 Entire class period		

Facility	Equipment	Organization
Walking route designed for the game	Instructions, containers for instructions (envelopes, sandwich bags, cans)	Entire class

 Watch where you are going.

Encourage students to walk at their best pace to keep the game moving.

 Design a route appropriate for your students.

Create instructions for students (see sample).

Hide instructions along the route.

Tell your class that (a) anyone who has any route information should share it with the entire class, and (b) the entire class must finish the walk as a group.

Give the first written instruction to any student.

Have students bring back instruction containers as they leave each station. (The instruction containers consist of sandwich bags and 3 x 5 cards with the clues written on them.)

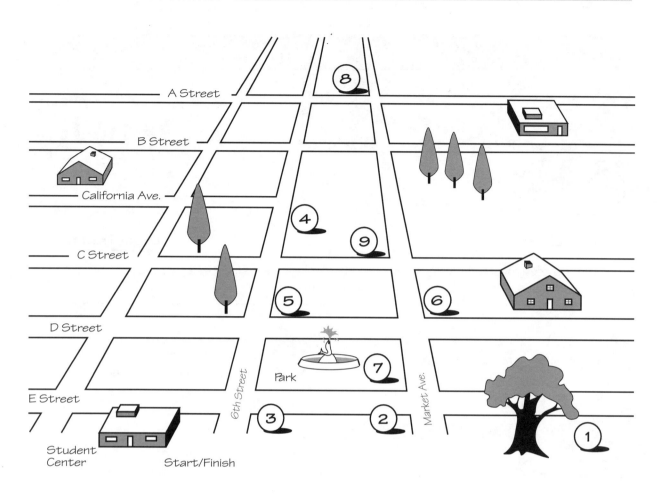

Sample Mad Scramble Clues

Clue received at start:	Go right on E Street to the biggest tree at the end of the street.
Clue received at 1:	Oops—wrong way! Go back on E to Market.
Clue received at 2:	Continue to 6th and E.
Clue received at 3:	Go up 6th to California.
Clue received at 4:	Wrong again! Go back down 6th to D.
Clue received at 5:	Take D to Market.
Clue received at 6:	You're right for once—congratulations! Go right on Market to the fountain in the park.
Clue received at 7:	You're off track again! Go back down Market to A.
Clue received at 8:	Wrong again! Go back up Market to C.
Clue received at 9:	Right on! Home to the Student Center!

Mad Scramble Worksheet

Name: _____ **Class:** _____ **Date:** _____

Questions

1. What made this game difficult?

2. How well did the first people to get to a clue share information?

3. What would you do to change this game?

From *Walking Games and Activities* by June Decker and Monica Mize, 2002, Champaign, IL: Human Kinetics.

Partner Relays

Type of Activity	Objectives	Grade Level

Entire class period.

Facility	Equipment	Organization
Measured laps in gymnasium, playing field, or indoor or outdoor track	Stopwatch, pencil, score sheet for every two students	Pairs

Stay in designated area.

Be aware of other walkers.

Group students in pairs.

Decide how long the relay should be for your group. Choose a half mile, a mile, or two miles (or the comparable metric distances such as 800, 1,500 or 3,000 meters). Tell students how many laps equal those distances.

Instruct students to take turns walking laps until they have completed the number of laps to equal a specified distance.

Have students time the laps.

Instruct students to take their heart rate after walking this distance and record it on the worksheet for each partner for each distance.

Have students record the other information indicated on the score sheet.

Partner Relays Worksheet

Name: _____ **Class:** _____ **Date:** _____

Distance to be walked: 1/2 mile (.8 kilometer)

Number of laps to be completed:	_____		
Individual 1 lap time:	_____	_____	_____
Individual 1 heart rate:	_____	_____	_____
Individual 2 lap time:	_____	_____	_____
Individual 2 heart rate:	_____	_____	_____
Total time for 1/2 mile (.8 kilometer)	_____		

Distance to be walked: 1 mile (1.6 kilometers)

Individual 1 lap time:	_____	_____	_____
Individual 1 heart rate:	_____	_____	_____
Individual 2 lap time:	_____	_____	_____
Individual 2 heart rate:	_____	_____	_____
Total time for 1 mile (1.6 kilometers)	_____		

Distance to be walked: 2 miles (3.2 kilometers)

Number of laps to be completed:	_____		
Individual 1 lap time:	_____	_____	_____
Individual 1 heart rate:	_____	_____	_____
Individual 2 lap time:	_____	_____	_____
Individual 2 heart rate:	_____	_____	_____
Total time for 2 mile (3.2 kilometers)	_____		

Questions

1. Did you enjoy doing this activity with a partner?

2. Did you find yourself competing against your partner's lap time?

3. Did you get bored during your partner's lap?

4. Did you encourage your partner to walk as fast as possible?

Comments:

From *Walking Games and Activities* by June Decker and Monica Mize, 2002, Champaign, IL: Human Kinetics.

Perceived Exertion

Type of Activity	Objectives	Grade Level
Approximately 45 minutes		

Facility	Equipment	Organization
Track or .2- to .25-mile (.32- to .4-kilometer) circle, gymnasium	Perceived exertion sheets, stopwatch, pencils	Individuals

Prerequisite Minilectures

Understanding Perceived Exertion
Taking Your Pulse
Calculating Your Target Heart Rate

 Don't run into anyone else.

 Give each student a perceived exertion worksheet.

Explain to the students that they will walk about .25 miles (.4 kilometers) at each of the five paces.

After the completion of each pace, students should record their heart rates.

Upon completion of all five paces, students should place an asterisk next to the paces at which they were in their target zone.

Perceived Exertion Worksheet

Name: _____ **Class:** _____ **Date:** _____

Pace	Heart rate
Very slow	
Slow	
Medium	
Fast	
Very fast	

Questions

1. What is the slowest pace you can go and be in your target heart rate range?

2. What is the fastest pace you can go and be in your target heart rate range?

3. How well do you think you can tell if you're in your target heart rate range by how fast you're walking?

From *Walking Games and Activities* by June Decker and Monica Mize, 2002, Champaign, IL: Human Kinetics.

Scavenger Hunt

Type of Activity	Objectives	Grade Level
		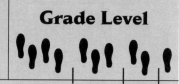

 Entire class period.

Facility	Equipment	Organization
Indoor or outdoor designated area	Items list, worksheets, pencils	Pairs or groups of three

 Stay within designated area.

 Choose 6 to 10 items (see sample items) that can be found within the designated area.

Prepare items list, making a copy for each team.

Divide class into pairs or groups of three.

Give each group the list of items to be found and a time by which they must return to the starting point.

When all teams return, compare items found. There will be a winning team for each item on the list. For example, the team with the signature of the person who has been on campus for the longest will win that item. Each team with the superlative of each item (oldest paper, biggest rock, signature of the person with the most tenure) receives one point for that item. The team returning first with all items receives two points. The team with the most cumulative points wins the game.

All teammates must stay together.

No running is allowed.

Sample Scavenger Hunt Items

(see page 131)

A signature from someone who has worked at the school more than 10 years

An old school newspaper

A black rock

A large leaf

A business card

A school sports schedule

A map of the campus

A short pencil

A piece of colored paper

Something with the school colors on it

signature

old school newspaper

large leaf

black rock

business card

map of campus

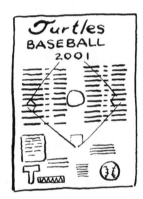

school sports schedule

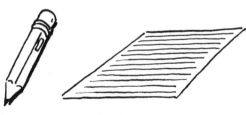

short
pencil

colored paper

pennant with
school colors

Scavenger Hunt Worksheet

Name: _____ **Class:** _____ **Date:** _____

Questions

1. Which item on the list was the easiest to find?

2. Which item was the hardest to find?

3. How well did you and your teammates work together?

4. How could you work better as a team?

5. How would you change this game?

From *Walking Games and Activities* by June Decker and Monica Mize, 2002, Champaign, IL: Human Kinetics.

Treasure Hunt

Type of Activity	Objectives	Grade Level

Entire class period.

Facility	Equipment	Organization
A somewhat circular route	Clues, containers for clues, pencils, worksheets	Pairs or groups of three

 Stay in your target heart rate range.

 Clues should be challenging but solvable.

 Design a somewhat circular route for your students.

Devise clues for students.

Hide clues along the route. At each site, place one copy of the clue for each team. Each clue should lead to the next site.

Divide class into pairs or groups of three.

Give clue 1 to team 1. Begin timing.

Exactly two minutes later, give clue 1 to team 2, and so on, starting teams at two-minute intervals until all teams have begun.

Students must solve the clue, walk to the site, and retrieve the next clue. The activity continues until a team has covered the entire route.

The team that solves all the clues in the least amount of time is the winner.

Teams must stay together, and no running is allowed.

Treasure Hunt Clues

Grocery store and wild animal (Market and Lyon)

Capitol of Wyoming and June (Cheyenne and 6th)

Home of Los Angeles and in between 1/7 and 1/9 (California and 8th)

A really bad grade and an Irish name (F and Kelly)

A bug and a university (B and College)

Where diamonds are a girl's best friend (softball field)

Venus and Serena play here (tennis courts)

Treasure Hunt Worksheet

Name: **Class:**   **Date:**

Questions

1. How hard do you believe you worked today?

2. How well did your team work together?

3. What could your team have done better?

4. How would you change this activity?

From *Walking Games and Activities* by June Decker and Monica Mize, 2002, Champaign, IL: Human Kinetics.

Walk, Crunch, and Jump Rope

Type of Activity	Objective	Grade Level 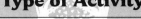

 Variable; 10 to 45 minutes depending on age and conditioning

Facility	Equipment	Organization
Indoor our outdoor track, gym, or other measured circular route	One pencil/pen per student, 10 to 15 jump ropes, one worksheet per student, stopwatch	Individual

Prerequisite Mini-lectures

Taking Your Pulse

Calculating Your Target Heart Rate

Stay in designated area for walking.

Find your own space for jumping rope.

Execute the activities with the correct techniques.

 First, have students walk around the designated area for one minute.

Next, have students jump rope for one minute.

Then have students execute crunches for one minute.

Afterward, have students take and record their heart rate.

Repeat the sequence as many times as possible in the designated time period.

Finally, have students complete the answers on the worksheet.

 Make sure students have basic jump-roping skills before doing the activity. Be sure to demonstrate the proper way to execute a crunch and give students time to practice it. The correct technique for executing a crunch is to lie on your back and bend your knees, with your feet close to your buttocks and your arms folded across your chest. Curl up until your shoulder blades lose contact with the floor. Return to the starting position and repeat.

 Vary order to see if that affects heart rate.

Walk, Crunch, and Jump Rope Worksheet

Name: _____ **Class:** _____ **Date:** _____

Record heart rate information and answer the following questions:

Resting heart rate: _____

Target heart rates: _____ 60 percent _____ 90 percent

Heart rate after each completed circuit:

Questions

1. How many circuits did you complete?

2. Did your heart rate increase with each circuit?

3. After which circuit was your heart rate the highest? The lowest?

4. Which part of the circuit did you find the most demanding (hardest to do)?

5. If you recorded your target heart rate limits, did your heart rate reach your target zone?

6. In how many circuits were you working in your target zone?

7. Did you enjoy this activity? Why or why not?

8. What did you learn from this activity?

From *Walking Games and Activities* by June Decker and Monica Mize, 2002, Champaign, IL: Human Kinetics.

Wheel

Type of Activity	Objectives	Grade Level

Entire class period

Facility	Equipment	Organization
Approximately circular route	Clues, containers for roll sheets, pencils, worksheets, and roll sheets	Pairs or groups of three

 Stay in designated area.

 Design an approximately circular route appropriate for your students.

Design clues to sites along the route.

Hide containers with roll sheets at designated sites.

Divide students into pairs or groups of three.

Give each group a number, as well as the clue to the site corresponding to their number. Team 1 gets the clue for site 1, team 2 gets the clue for site 2, and so on.

Teams are to solve the clue, walk to the site, have all team members sign the roll sheet, and then return the roll sheet and container to their place.

The team then returns to the teacher to get the next clue. Team 1 now gets clue 2, and so on.

The team that solves all clues, walks to all sites, and returns to the teacher first wins the game.

Groups must stay together.

No running is allowed.

 The game can also be played indoors (see indoor clues).

 Tell students that if they figure out why the game is called Wheel, it might help them be successful.

Sample Wheel Clues

Andre and Venus are supreme here (tennis courts)

Old things live here (museum)

N, S, __, W and an Irish name (E and Kelly)

Sample Indoor Wheel Clues

Do you want to lose some? (weight room)

Have you won any awards? (trophy case)

Are you hungry? (concessions)

Wheel Worksheet

Name: _____ **Class:** _____ **Date:** _____

Questions

1. How well did you cooperate in solving clues?

2. How well did you listen to the opinions of your teammates?

3. What should you have done differently?

4. How would you change this game?

From *Walking Games and Activities* by June Decker and Monica Mize, 2002, Champaign, IL: Human Kinetics.

Where in the World?

Type of Activity	Objectives	Grade Level
One class period		

Facility	Equipment	Organization
Campus	Activity sheets, pencils, worksheets	Pairs or groups of three

Stay in designated area.

Choose items that students can find without disrupting other classes.

Find interesting or unusual items on your campus.

Prepare activity sheets (see sample).

Divide students into pairs or groups of three.

Each group is to walk to the places or find the items on the activity sheet. When they reach their destination, they must write down exactly where the item is. (Example: Library, third floor, last row, fifth book from the left on the top shelf.)

The team that returns to the starting point first after finding all the items is the winner.

Group members must stay together.

No running is allowed.

Where in the World? Worksheet (Sample)

Where is there a bench with the year 1908 on it?

Where is there a picture of the 1924 women's basketball team?

Where is there a June 1, 1957, copy of the school newspaper?

Where is there an XL-sized new school T-shirt?

Where is there a live reptile?

Where in the World? Worksheet

Name: _____ **Class:** _____ **Date:** _____

Questions

1. What did you learn about your campus today?

2. Describe how you and your partner(s) worked together.

3. What did you do that worked well?

4. What could you have done better?

From *Walking Games and Activities* by June Decker and Monica Mize, 2002, Champaign, IL: Human Kinetics.

Walk Talk

Type of Activity	Objectives	Grade Level

Facility	Equipment	Organization
Classroom or gymnasium	Walk Talk Challenge terms and definitions, score sheets, pencils	Teacher and class

From 20 minutes to the entire class period

 Divide the words into point categories of 1, 5, 10, 15, and 20.

Randomly select a student to choose a point category.

All students write the point value beside the corresponding challenge on the answer sheet.

Read the definition aloud, and the students write the correct response on the blank provided on the answer sheet.

At the end of the game, read the correct answers to each challenge. Students will total the number of points they answered correctly.

The student(s) with the highest score at the end of the game wins.

 Put students in teams and play Walk Talk Challenge as a team activity. The team with the highest combined score would be the winner.

 This is a good activity for a rainy day, for a shortened schedule, or at anytime throughout the walking unit to introduce new terms or review previously learned terms with the students.

Adjust the vocabulary words to match the developmental level of the students.

Walking Terms

Aerobic: The ability to supply the oxygen needed while exercising.

Cool-down: Light activity followed by stretching, allowing the body systems to slow down gradually.

Cross-training: Workout program that employs a variety of activities rather than just one.

Diminishing returns: The more fit one is, the harder it is to make a big improvement.

Fat: The secondary source of energy for the body.

Fitness walking: A type of walking that produces health and fitness benefits because one is exercising within one's target heart rate zone.

Flexibility: Capacity of a joint to move through its range of motion.

Frequency: How often one does an activity.

Goal: Objective that one wants to achieve.

Health-related fitness: Fitness programs that focus on the development of aerobics, muscular strength, muscular endurance, and flexibility.

Intensity: How hard one works at an activity.

Minerals: Basic chemical elements used in the body to help form body structure and regulate body processes.

Muscular strength: The amount of force a muscle can produce.

Obesity: 25 to 30 percent body fat.

Overload: Doing more exercise or activity than normal to improve fitness.

Overweight: Excessive weight for one's height.

Perceived exertion: Awareness of whether one is in one's target heart rate range based on how the body feels.

Progression: Continuing to increase workload from light to moderate.

Protein: Used for growth and rebuilding of tissue.

Pulse: Number of times the heart beats per minute.

Race walking: Competitive form of walking that requires specific techniques to be within the rules.

Reversibility: Loss of the benefits gained after one stops participating in an activity.

Shin splints: Pain around the front or either side of the lower leg bone resulting from inflammation.

Specificity: Activities and exercise are specific and limited to the parts of the body that are worked on regularly.

Stress: An emotional, mental, and/or physical response to some external demand or event in one's life.

Target zone: The heart rate range necessary to achieve cardiorespiratory improvement.

Time: How long one participates in an activity.

Vitamins: Compounds needed in very small amounts in the diet to help support and regulate chemical reactions in the body.

Warm-up: The beginning component of a workout that prepares the body for more vigorous activity.

Water: Provides the medium for nutrients and waste transport.

Sample Score Sheet

Name: _____ **Class:** _____ **Date:** _____

Challenge #	Point value	Answer	Points for correct answer
1	20	aerobic	20
2	5	frequency	0
3	10	heart rate	10
4	1	pulse	1
5	1	fitness	0
			Total points scored: 31

Walk Talk Worksheet

Name: **Class:**   **Date:**

Questions

1. How many points did your team score?

2. Write a short story using the names of all your classmates and at least 15 of your walking terms.

From *Walking Games and Activities* by June Decker and Monica Mize, 2002, Champaign, IL: Human Kinetics.

Walking Bingo

Type of Activity	Objectives	Grade Level

From 10 to 20 minutes depending on number of games played

Facility	Equipment	Organization
Classroom or gymnasium	Game sheet per student, call words, and markers (paper clips, pennies, beans)	Teacher, class

Before Play

Photocopy the vocabulary words on the call word cutout sheets. You also can use the sample call word cutout sheet to fill in your own vocabulary words relevant to your particular activity.

Make copies of the blank game sheet and randomly fill in the squares with vocabulary words from the call word cutout sheets (see sample game sheets). Make sure each game sheet is different so each student has a unique sheet.

Cut out the call words by cutting along the lines on the call word sheets.

Tell the students the rules of the game.

Decide who will be the caller.

Have the caller shuffle the call words and place them face down.

Have each player choose a game sheet and take several markers.

Play

Each player begins by covering the free space with a marker. The caller draws the first call word from the stack and announces it to the players. Each player whose game sheet has that word on it covers it with a marker. The caller then puts that

word aside (not back in the stack) and draws and announces the next word. The game continues until one player has covered a row of words (horizontally, vertically, or diagonally), all four corners, or the entire card, depending on the game choice, and that player wins the game. That player calls "Walking Bingo" and reads back the words so that the caller may check them against the words that have been called. The winner of each game becomes the next caller. In case of a tie, the person with the most words covered is declared the winner.

Have the students copy the words on their bingo sheet on a separate sheet of paper and, for their homework assignment, use each of those words in a sentence.

Have the students copy the words on their bingo sheet on a separate sheet of paper and write the definitions of the words. All the definitions can be put together to make a walking bingo dictionary.

Tell students not to clear their card until instructed to do so in case another game variation could continue to be played.

Walking Bingo Call Words

(Cut along the lines)

Heart	Weight	Health	Performance
Speed	Progress	Overload	Power
Activity	Technique	Goals	Endurance
Heredity	Pace	Distance	Nutrition

From *Walking Games and Activities* by June Decker and Monica Mize, 2002, Champaign, IL: Human Kinetics.

Walking Bingo Call Words

(Cut along the lines)

Injury	Activities	Progression	Fun
Lifestyles	Calories	Age	Surfaces
Workouts	Lungs	Rewards	Body composition
Neck	Breathing	Carbohydrates	Back

From *Walking Games and Activities* by June Decker and Monica Mize, 2002, Champaign, IL: Human Kinetics.

Walking Bingo Call Words

(Cut along the lines)

Cardiorespiratory	Conditioning	Route	Shoulders
Vitamins	Overload	Posture	Stress
Aerobic	Exercise	Form	Intensity
Frequency	Shin	Respiratory	Race

From *Walking Games and Activities* by June Decker and Monica Mize, 2002, Champaign, IL: Human Kinetics.

Walking Bingo Call Words

(Cut along the lines)

Shoes	Strength	Habit	Prevention
Warm-ups	Muscles	Attitude	Behavior
Events	Weight	Variety	Exercise
Flexibility	Fitness	Trunk	Thighs

From *Walking Games and Activities* by June Decker and Monica Mize, 2002, Champaign, IL: Human Kinetics.

Walking Bingo Call Words

(Cut along the lines)

Water	Ankles	Minerals	Specificity
Exertion	Fat	Cooperation	Competition
Pace	Abdominal	Pedometer	Obesity
Wellness	Safety	Benefits	Arm swing

From *Walking Games and Activities* by June Decker and Monica Mize, 2002, Champaign, IL: Human Kinetics.

Walking Bingo Call Words

(Cut along the lines)

Bones	Cool-down	Physical	Motivation
Routine	Energy	Stretching	Training
Posture	Pulse	Program	Cross-training
Oxygen	Repetition	Duration	Low impact

Walking Bingo Playing Card

Heart	Weight	Health	Performance
Speed	Progress	Walk free space	Power
Activity	Technique	Goals	Endurance
Heredity	Pace	Distance	Nutrition

From *Walking Games and Activities* by June Decker and Monica Mize, 2002, Champaign, IL: Human Kinetics.

Walking Bingo Playing Card

Aerobic	Exercise	Attitude	Weight
Variety	Anaerobic	Shoes	Fitness
Benefits	Bones	Back	Rewards
Walk free space	Power	Health	Speed

From *Walking Games and Activities* by June Decker and Monica Mize, 2002, Champaign, IL: Human Kinetics.

Walking Bingo Playing Card

		Walk free space	

From *Walking Games and Activities* by June Decker and Monica Mize, 2002, Champaign, IL: Human Kinetics.

Walking Bingo Worksheet

Name: _____ **Class:** _____ **Date:** _____

Select 10 words from your bingo score sheet and write them on the lines below. For tomorrow's homework assignment, look up each word in a dictionary and write the definition of each word. Next use each of the words defined in a sentence.

Word: _____

    Definition:

    Sentence:

Word: _____

    Definition:

    Sentence:

Word: _____

    Definition:

    Sentence:

Word: _____

    Definition:

    Sentence:

Word: _____

    Definition:

    Sentence:

From *Walking Games and Activities* by June Decker and Monica Mize, 2002, Champaign, IL: Human Kinetics.

Word: _____

    Definition:

    Sentence:

Word: _____

    Definition:

    Sentence:

Word: _____

    Definition:

    Sentence:

Word: _____

    Definition:

    Sentence:

Word: _____

    Definition:

    Sentence:

Write a story using all of the words listed above.

Walking Spelling Bee

Type of Activity	Objective	Grade Level
Entire class period.		

Facility	Equipment	Organization
Classroom or gymnasium	List of spelling words and a stopwatch	Teacher class formation

 Distribute a list of spelling words to the students.

Announce a date for the spelling bee in advance.

Describe the rules and regulations for the spelling bee to the students.

Conduct the spelling bee.

Announce the winners and present awards (certificates, T-shirt, trophy, bonus points).

Give out a certain number of spelling words each day and hold the spelling bee at the end of the unit.

This activity is suitable for a rainy day, shortened schedule day, or end-of-unit activity. You may incorporate walking by holding a practice session in which students walk a lap for each letter in the spelling word.

Walking Spelling Bee Word List

Abdomen	Lifestyle
Activities	Minerals
Activity	Motivation
Aerobic	Muscles
Anaerobic	Nutrition
Ankles	Obesity
Arm swing	Overload
Attitude	Pedometer
Back	Performance
Behavior	Physical
Benefits	Posture
Body composition	Power
Breathing	Prevention
Calories	Program
Calves	Progress
Carbohydrates	Progression
Cardiorespiratory	Respiratory
Competition	Rewards
Cool-down	Routine
Cooperation	Safety
Distance	Shoulders
Endurance	Specificity
Energy	Specificity weight
Event	Strength
Exercise	Stress
Exertion	Stretching
Fat	Surfaces
Fitness	Technique
Flexibility	Thighs
Frequency	Training
Health	Variety
Heart	Vitamins
Heredity	Warm-up
Injury	Weight
Intensity	Wellness
Interval	Workouts

Walking Spelling Bee Worksheet

Name: _____ **Class:** _____ **Date:** _____

Fill in the blank with a word from the spelling bee list.

The ability to supply the oxygen needed for exercise while one is exercising _____

Light activity followed by stretching, allowing the body systems to return to normal _____

Workout program that employs several activities rather than just one _____

The secondary source of energy for the body_____

Capacity of a joint to move through its range of motion_____

How hard you work _____

Doing more exercise or activity than normal to improve fitness _____

Provides the medium for nutrients and waste transport _____

From *Walking Games and Activities* by June Decker and Monica Mize, 2002, Champaign, IL: Human Kinetics.

Walking Training Programs

General Principles

Always alternate hard days and easy days.

Spend more time on form than on speed.

Interval train once per week.

Always take one day off per week.

Sample Programs

Here are some sample training programs for students who want to compete in walking races:

400-Meter Race Program

Monday—1 mile (1.6 kilometers), restful pace, work on form

Tuesday—intervals, 4 × 100 meters, 80 percent effort

Wednesday—1 mile (1.6 kilometers), restful pace, work on form

Thursday—500 meters, 70 percent effort

Friday—1 mile (1.6 kilometers), restful pace, work on form

Saturday—2 miles (3.2 kilometers), slow pace

Sunday—rest

1,500-Meter Race Program

Monday—1.5 miles (2.4 kilometers), restful pace, work on form

Tuesday—intervals, 4 × 200 meters, 80 percent effort

Wednesday—1.5 miles (2.4 kilometers), restful pace, work on form

Thursday—1 mile (1.6 kilometers), 70 percent effort

Friday—1.5 miles (2.4 kilometers), restful pace, work on form

Saturday—3 miles (4.8 kilometers), slow pace

Sunday—rest

5K Race Program

Monday—1.5 miles (2.4 kilometers), restful pace

Tuesday—3 miles (4.8 kilometers), 70 percent effort

Wednesday—1.5 miles (2.4 kilometers), restful pace

Thursday—2 miles (3.2 kilometers), 70 percent effort

Friday—1.5 miles (2.4 kilometers), restful pace

Saturday—4 miles (6.4 kilometers), slow pace

Sunday—rest

10K Race Program

Monday—3 miles (4.8 kilometers)

Tuesday—5 miles (8 kilometers) or 6 × 400-meter intervals

Wednesday—3 miles (4.8 kilometers)

Thursday—4 miles (6.4 kilometers); 5 miles (8 kilometers) if you did intervals on Tuesday

Friday—3 miles (4.8 kilometers)

Saturday—8 miles (12.9 kilometers)

Sunday—rest

20K Race Program

Same as 10K program except on Saturday per month do a 10- to 13-mile (16- to 20.9-kilometer) slow walk.

Conversions

Just a reminder . . .

1 kilometer = .62 miles

1 meter = 1.09 yards

Walking Log

Name: _____

Target Heart Rate Range _____ **Low** _____ **High**

Date	Route	Time	Distance	Comments
_____	_____	_____	_____	_____
_____	_____	_____	_____	_____
_____	_____	_____	_____	_____
_____	_____	_____	_____	_____
_____	_____	_____	_____	_____
_____	_____	_____	_____	_____
_____	_____	_____	_____	_____
_____	_____	_____	_____	_____
_____	_____	_____	_____	_____
_____	_____	_____	_____	_____

From *Walking Games and Activities* by June Decker and Monica Mize, 2001, Champaign, IL: Human Kinetics.

For More Walking Information

Books

Davis, Kathryn L. (1997). *Fitness Walking Everyone.* Winston-Salem, NC: Hunter Textbooks.

Floyd, Patricia A., and Parke, Janet E. (1996). *Walk, Jog, Run for Wellness Everyone.* Winston-Salem, NC: Hunter Textbooks.

Getchell, Bud, Mikesky, Alan E., and Mikesky, Kay N. (1998). *Physical Fitness, A Way of Life.* Needham Heights, MA: Allyn & Bacon.

Hawkins, Jerald D., and Weigle, Sandra M. (1992). *Walking for Fun & Fitness.* Englewood, CO: Morton Publishing.

Hawkins, Jerald D., and Hawkins, Sandra M. (1996). *Walking for Fitness,* second edition. Englewood, CO: Morton Publishing Company.

Prentice, William. (1994). *Fitness for College and Life,* fourth edition. St. Louis: Mosby-Yearbook.

Rosato, Frank. (1995). *Jogging and Walking for Health and Fitness,* third edition. Englewood, CO: Morton Publishing.

Seiger, Lon H., and Hesson, James. (1998). *Walking for Fitness,* third edition. St. Louis: WCB/McGraw-Hill Publishers.

Journals

The Walking Magazine, P.O. Box 52341, Boulder, CO 80321-2341.

Volksport Monthly, 5101 NE 121st Avenue, #75, Vancouver, WA 98682.

Walking Journal, Box 454, Athens, GA 30603.

Organizations

American Alliance for Health, Physical Education, Recreation and Dance, 1900 Association Drive, Reston, VA 20191.

American Heart Association, National Center, 7372 Greenville Avenue, Dallas, TX 75231.

American Volksport Association, 1001 Pat Booker Road, Suite 101, University City, TX 78148.

International Walking Society, P.O. Box 4037, Boulder, CO 80306.

National Association of Mall Walkers, P.O. Box 191, Herman, MO 65041.

Walking Association, 655 Rancho Cataline Place, Tucson, AZ 86704.

Walkways Center, 733 15th Street NW, Suite 427, Washington, DC 20005.

Web Sites

All Health Fitness
www.allhealth.com
American College of Sports Medicine
www.acsm.org
American Council on Exercise
www.acefitness.org
Dynamic Health and Fitness
www.dynamicwalking.com
Focus on Fitness for Seniors
www.eldernet.com/fitness.htm
Health for the Whole Woman
www.herhealth.com
Health Walk to Fitness
www.healthwalk.com
Hunter Textbooks Inc.
www.huntertextbooks.com/links.htm
i Village Diet and Fitness
www.ivillage.com

McGraw–Hill Higher Education
www.mhhe.com
Office Workouts, Inc.
www.officeworkouts.com
Shape Up America
www.shapeup.org
Sports Music
www.sportsmusic.com
Teleport Internet Services
www.teleport.com
The New Health Thrive On Line
www.thriveonline.com
UC Davis Health System Wellness Center
wellness.ucdavis.edu
Walkable Communities, Inc.
www.walkable.org
Walking Magazine
www.walkingmag.com
Walking Organization
www.walking.org

About the Authors

June I. Decker is a professor and chair of wellness and movement sciences at Western New Mexico University. She has taught walking for more than 10 years and has been a competitive race walker for more than 15 years.

Decker received a PhD in curriculum and instruction in physical education from the University of New Mexico in 1985. A member of the American Alliance for Health, Physical Education, Recreation and Dance (AAHPERD), she is former secretary of its Southwest District and a member and former president of the New Mexico Association for Health, Physical Education, Recreation and Dance (NMAHPERD). In 1999 Decker received a Southwest District AAHPERD Honor Award and the NMAHPERD Professional Achievement Award. She is also chair of the Board of Directors of New Mexico Senior Olympics.

Decker has delivered numerous presentations at the local, state, regional, and national levels—but she believes that her most important accomplishment is her teaching. A resident of Silver City, New Mexico, she enjoys hiking and playing golf and tennis.

Monica G. Mize is a professor of health promotion and human performance and director of the physical education teaching program at Weber State University in Ogden, Utah. She has been a walking for fitness instructor for six years and has taught physical education for more than 20 years at every level from kindergarten through university.

Mize holds a PhD in physical education with an emphasis in curriculum and instructional strategies, which she received from Southern Illinois University in 1977. AAHPERD's Southwest District has presented her with an Honor Award (2000) and President's Service Award (1998), and she has received multiple awards from the AAHPERD state associations in Utah and Arizona. Mize has served as president of all three organizations. She also received Grambling State University's College of Education Research Award, Teaching/Service Award, and Teacher of the Year Award in 1988.

An advocate for physical education and active lifestyles, Mize has made individual and joint presentations on walking at local, state, district, and national conferences. In her spare time she enjoys walking, hiking, backpacking, and playing golf.

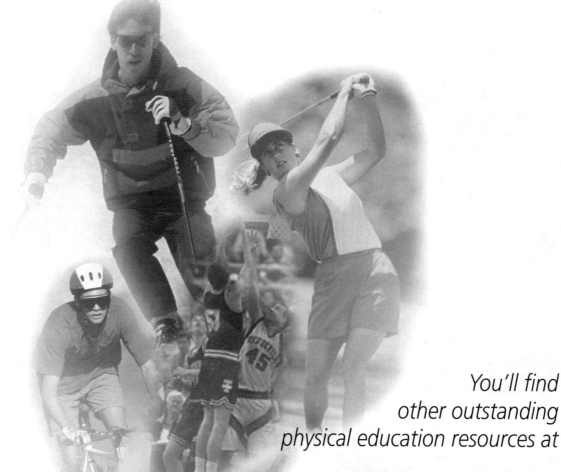